WILLIAM COOPER:
Death Of A Conspiracy Salesman

Survivalist?

Patriot?

FANATIC!

TOP SECRET
MAJESTYTWELVE
EYES ONLY

ANNUIT COEPTIS
NOVUS ORDO SECLORUM

EDITED BY COMMANDER X

GLOBAL COMMUNICATIONS

WILLIAM COOPER: DEATH OF A CONSPIRACY SALESMAN

Edited By Commander X

ISBN-10: 1892062305
ISBN-13: 978-1892062307

Editor: Timothy Green Beckley
Publishers Assistant: Carol Ann Rodriguez
Editorial Assistant: Sean Casteel
Cover Art: Tim R. Swartz

Global Communications
P.O. Box 753
New Brunswick, NJ 08903

Email: mrufo8@hotmail.com

A free weekly subscription to CONSPIRACY JOURNAL awaits you at: www.conspiracyjournal.com

WILLIAM COOPER: DEATH OF A CONSPIRACY SALESMAN

CONTENTS

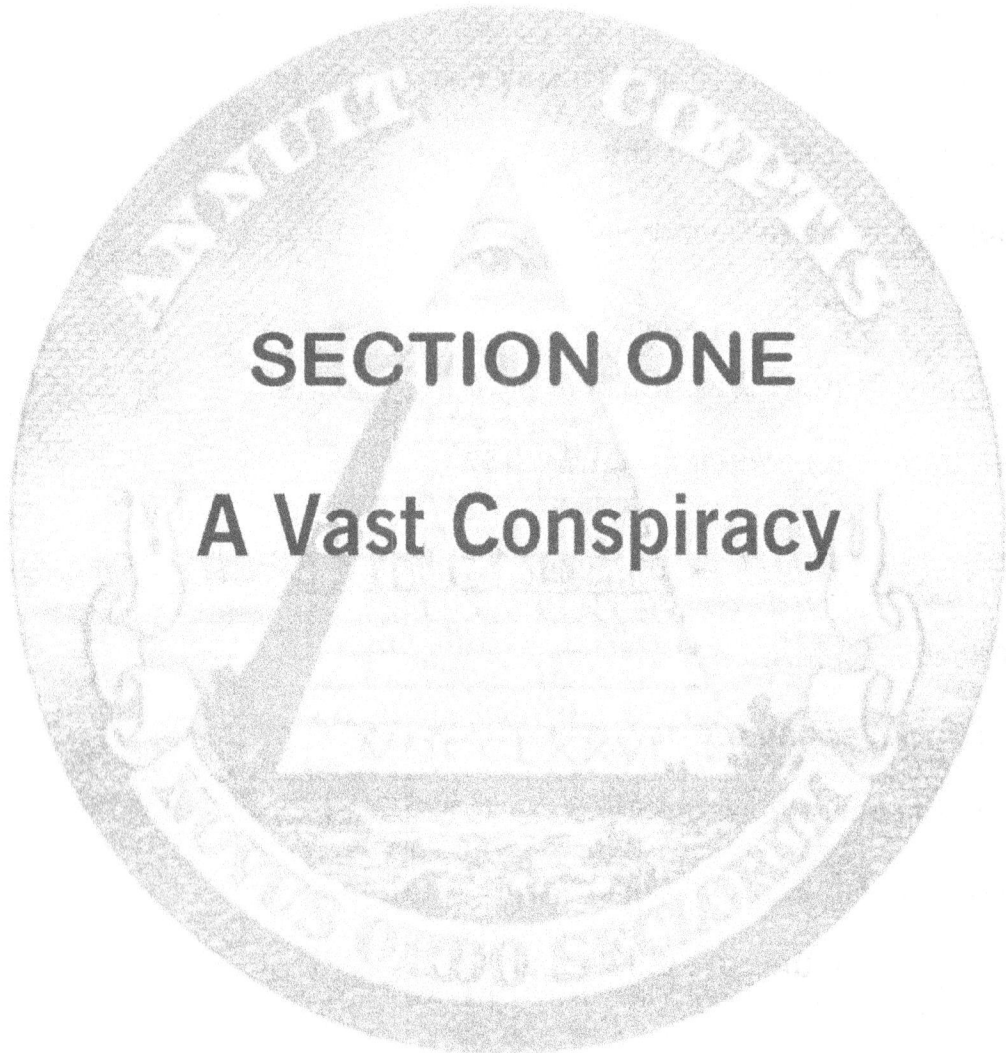

SECTION ONE

A Vast Conspiracy

WILLIAM COOPER: DEATH OF A CONSPIRACY SALESMAN

Dark Days Ahead

It hasn't been a good time for those who investigate the dark world of conspiracies and cover-ups. Even though public opinion tends to look unfavorably on writers and publishers of conspiracy theories - recent mass media revelations of top-secret projects, such as the communication-eavesdropping Echelon and Carnivore, can be originally accredited to the very same conspiracy-investigators considered too "far-out" by the popular press. However, it seems that someone else has become interested in the conspiracy-investigators - someone with a deadly interest.

Even though it may be just coincidence, recently there has been a series of unusual deaths and accidents involving investigators, writers, lecturers, and now, a publisher of conspiracy- theories. Investigative reporter Danny Casolaro, lecturer Phillip Schneider, writer Jim Keith and publisher Ron Bonds, all died under unusual circumstances.

In 2001, writer and researcher Branton, known for his book *The Dulce Wars* (1999, Global Communications), was critically injured in a mysterious hit-and-run accident. Suffering critical head-injuries, Branton remained in a coma for several weeks, but finally regained consciousness thanks to the efforts of his parents and worldwide fans.

Now another prominent person in the weird world of conspiracies has left this world in less than usual circumstances. But is the death of William Milton Cooper the result of a conspiracy to silence those who strive to make a complacent world aware of the evil that lies just underneath the veneer of our society - or simply the death of a man whose acquaintances had always known would end his life in violence and bloodshed?

On November 5, 2001, William Cooper was shot to death by sheriff deputies in an exchange of gunfire, fulfilling his often-stated wish to go out in a blaze of glory.

News of Cooper's death spread quickly via the Internet, as friend and foe alike posted letters describing their past, often confrontational, encounters with Cooper. Little surprise was expressed of the violent way in which his life had ended. Considering the way William Cooper lived, death in a hail of bullets was thought almost mandatory for the always outspoken author and radio-show host.

But just who was Milton William Cooper? UFO-expert? Conspiracy theorist? Anti-government militia madman? Survivalist? Patriot? Fanatic? William Cooper claimed to be one of the most knowledgeable experts in the field of "conspiracy science," the Illuminati, Freemasons, UFOs and the New

WILLIAM COOPER: DEATH OF A CONSPIRACY SALESMAN

World Order. He was a longtime critic of the Warren Commission Report and JFK Cover-up.

He was a U.S. Navy veteran who rendered many years of "Silent Service" on submarines and in Naval Intelligence. He was a man that many say was someone who did his duty as a "patriot" as he saw fit. Others say that Cooper was a vicious liar and opportunist who often threatened violence with his ever-present handgun. Although the media called Cooper a "national militia leader," no one has yet to come forward who was under his command, nor has anyone to this point come forward to claim his 'militia rank.'

Misguided though he may have been at times, Cooper always said he acted from his "conscience" and sought to warn all Americans of the dangers of the New World Order, creeping Socialism, and Nazism in America.

WILLIAM COOPER: DEATH OF A CONSPIRACY SALESMAN

WILD BILL
By Timothy Green Beckley

I had to drive 40 miles to meet him - straight out of Phoenix and down the long highway that heads towards Sedona and Flagstaff. But my turn off was not a major highway marker. Bill didn't like to drive the main roads. He said he was afraid and so he tried to stick close to home to protect his family (his Asian wife Anna had just given birth to a beautiful baby girl who I later saw cradled in her arms in the front parlor of Bill's home).

Just how afraid was he...and what was he afraid of?

Our rendezvous point was the Dairy Queen outside of Verde, Arizona. My instructions were to drive behind the structure and park my car. In a few minutes Bill pulled up to me and we met for the first time to shake hands.

Coop as I later came to refer to him was a big bear of a guy. Not fat mind you - just kind of stocky and "well worn" around the edges. He said I should slide into the front seat next to him and we would take off to talk at his home. Trying to erode some of the mystery about our encounter, Bill said that he lived on a street with no name (common in this neck of the woods - or desert I should say!) and liked it that way, mainly because none of his many detractors could find him easily.

He said he had been threatened numerous times and there had been an attempt to drive him off the road and assassinate him a few weeks before my visit. The only identification mark for Bill's residence was a rather beat up old Chevy parked at a helter-skelter angle across the "lawn" in front of the properly.

As we drove the back roads out of the Daily Queen, I got the impression that Coop was a bit paranoid about meeting anyone. He admitted that he pretty much liked to work in seclusion (he never headed a militia movement as the press indicated after his death).

The thing that sticks out in my mind about our first meeting was an item on the front seat between us - a revolver in a holster, right out in the open.

Reflecting on this, I kind of got the impression that Bill was trying, in a sense, to yank my chain. I felt he wanted me to believe he was "ready for anything" should we be confronted by "evil" along the way. Obviously, Bill's thinking was two sided. The pistol might well have been meant as a means of protection, but I always believed he thought it would fortify his "tough guy" image in my mind. Being a city slicker he probably didn't realize I knew it was common - and perfectly legal!

For an unconcealed gun to be displayed. Hell, as you walk through the streets, six shooters can still be seen strapped to the legs of "cowboys" who live in the area. So to have one in a holster on the seat of the car is pretty much meaningless - except as a fashion statement!

We sat in the well lit front parlor across from each other - eyeball to eyeball. A powerful spokesperson, Cooper alleged that not only is there an CIA-alien link, but that we are being controlled by a "Secret Government" who is responsible for feeding us false information on a variety of subjects and trying to distract our lives for their own sinister motives that many of us can only guess at!

One of the things that was obvious from the start was Bill's pre-occupation with the Constitution and the Bill of Rights and that such things as the UFO cover-up "violates every law that has ever been written."

He told me that it was his responsibility "to expose the conspiracy as thoroughly and as quickly as possible." He said his beliefs and outspokenness had put him in harms way numerous times and had to move repeatedly, change his address in order to keep a low profile.

At the time of our initial meet Cooper was all out in favor of the interplanetary origin for UFOs. He even proclaimed that he had seen documents proving that our government had actually ratified a treaty with the ETs to exchange their technology for human abductees. It was this discovery that set Cooper's belief system for years to come, utterly convinced that the government had set us up and had committed treasons to the citizens of the United States. That day I spent more than three hours with Bill in his home. He seem rational, clear thinking, reasonable at ease and certainly very devoted to his wife and little baby. I can't say I away believed his accounts hook, line and sinker, but I was willing to give him the benefit of the doubt.

Over the next few years I found my confidence in what he had to say to be on shaky ground. Repeatedly he changed his stories and eventually said that he had been duped into believing that UFOs were interplanetary and had changed his mind. He said he had new evidence that what we were seeing in the sky was really a super-secret technology that had been developed by Nazi scientists during the closing days of World War II. And that elements of the military had provided a safe haven for these scientists in the U.S. where the technology was further perfected at bases like Area 51 in the Nevada desert unseen by the prying eyes of the public.

Cooper spoke before large audiences at several of the UFO/Conspiracy conferences I had organized in Phoenix, Arizona. His workshops were filled to capacity (one of them lasted over 4 hours in the hundred degree heat; the air conditioning being over powered by the 150 people crammed into a small room), the gatherings profitable to both of us.

WILLIAM COOPER: DEATH OF A CONSPIRACY SALESMAN

Then one day shortly before one of his scheduled appearances at one of my programs, Cooper left a message on my answering machine...a very disturbing message that left me in a bind. He was refusing to come to the show because he felt I was acting as an agent of the IRS! The real story was that we had done so well that as a promoter and sponsor I naturally had to report his income on a W2 form as any business would do. While I have no reason to doubt Cooper sincerely felt he was not obligated to pay tax under what he saw as an unlawful amendment, I did not feel it my responsibility to avoid sending him the necessary paper work and possibly getting into "trouble" with the IRS.

I don't believe I ever spoke to Bill after he backed out of an appearance that had been heavily advertised - especially, since I had helped promote previous engagements and more successfully then most other sponsors he had worked with.

But that's water under the dam. Perhaps we will never know the real Bill Cooper as he did not welcome the opportunity to open himself up to others. Perhaps others knew him better than I did, and ultimately his work will have to stand on its own. History will tell how "on track" he was in his pronouncements. And God save us all!!!

"Mr UFO" Timothy Green Beckley

1.

William Cooper: Target For The New World Order?

Bill Cooper had always known that they would come for him someday. They would come for him because he knew too much, and would not, could not, keep to himself the terrifying truth that he had uncovered. He had known that he was a wanted man by the secret government and those who were involved with the ultimate conspiracy. He knew the frightening truth, and through his shortwave radio broadcasts and Internet website, he tried to warn the rest of the country about the evil men who sought total, absolute control of all of mankind.

They had tried to come for him before. Representatives of the puppet government too stupid to realize that their entire lives were a sham. But Cooper was always ready for them. He never left home without his pistol; he never knew when he would have to use it for that final time. He knew it was inevitable.

William Cooper was no stranger to controversy. He was one of the first to publicly announce that there was a government cover-up concerning UFOs. At first, Cooper, along with John Lear and others, was convinced that the United States government had fallen into an unholy alliance with extraterrestrial creatures, with the innocent citizens of planet Earth as their unwitting pawns. He would later change his mind and declare that the whole "extraterrestrials in league with the U.S. government" was a massive disinformation campaign by the New World Order.

The aliens did not exist. Instead, the entire UFO phenomenon was masterminded by secret societies in control of the worlds governments. High-technology, but strictly man made, secret aircraft were deliberately used to fool the public that UFOs were alien spacecraft. Many were convinced that it was this revelation that made Bill Cooper a wanted man.

On November 5, 2001, the silent night around the Cooper house was suddenly shattered by the sound of loud music, laughter, and the grinding cacophony of pickup truck engines. It wasn't the first time that teenagers, looking for a secluded place to party had parked on the road leading to the house. And like before, Bill grabbed his gun and got into his car, heading down the lane to chase the intruders away.

However, these intruders were not who they seemed, and they were waiting for Cooper. They knew what he was ready to do. What he had always said he would do. And they knew what they had to do. All they needed was for Cooper to make the first move.

WILLIAM COOPER: DEATH OF A CONSPIRACY SALESMAN

Militia Leader William Cooper Killed Deputy Critical In Shootout
The Arizona Republic 11-6-1

EAGER, AZ - A national leader of the militia movement has been killed and an Apache County sheriff's deputy wounded in a shootout, authorities said.

William Milton Cooper, 58, of Eager, had hosted a talk show broadcast on the Worldwide Christian Radio out of Nashville, which receives it via phone from his home in St. Johns. He had millions of listeners worldwide, including Timothy McVeigh.

The deputy, whose name was being withheld by authorities, was shot twice in the head while trying to arrest Cooper, a state Department of Public Safety spokesman said today. Cooper was killed by another officer.

Several deputies were attempting to arrest Cooper, who was armed with a handgun, said Officer Steve Volden, a spokesman for the DPS, which was investigating the shooting. He said details of the shooting would be released later today. The deputy was in critical condition at a Phoenix hospital early today, Volden said.

Cooper was one of the most widely known prophets of the "patriot movement," railing at the federal government and talking of doomsday omens in his radio broadcast.

McVeigh, who was executed in May for the bombing of the federal building in Oklahoma City, listened to Cooper's broadcasts for inspiration, according to testimony by James Nichols, brother of Oklahoma bombing co-defendant Terry Nichols during a 1996 pretrial hearing.

Like some other patriot leaders, Cooper refused to get a driver's license or pay federal income taxes, saying he is willing to risk getting ticketed and has found a legal way to avoid the taxes.

The patriot movement grew during the 1990s, fed by a series of news events - the siege of Randy Weaver in Idaho, the raid on the Branch Davidians near Waco, Texas and the signing of gun-control laws.

"He has been claiming ever since the Income Tax situation that he wouldn't be taken alive, and evidently he was a man of his word."
Anonymous e-mail

"...God bless my family. I love my wife & children more than life itself. Everything I do is for the future of all my children. They may not understand why I have sacrificed so much, why I am so dedicated to this work; but someday they will. I want them to know they are the most important People in my life, and how very, very much I love them..."
William Cooper

WILLIAM COOPER: DEATH OF A CONSPIRACY SALESMAN

FROM WEBMASTER - www.williamcooper.com Updated: Tuesday, November 6th, 2001, 2:20 PM

With a deep sense of loss and mourning we announce the passing of William Cooper

It appears at this time to be totally unrelated to the disputes he had with the federal government. All we know at this time is that he was shot and killed by an Apache County Sheriff around 12:15 AM this morning while serving of an arrest warrant on a local issue. A sheriff was also wounded.

Remain Calm! This is in no way a cause for action, but all patriots should be on high alert at this time. Do NOT listen to or spread undocumented and unconfirmed RUMORS! If it is not here it is not confirmed as fact. Updates will be posted here as they become available.

We MUST all remember his love of freedom, America, the Constitution and the values it is founded on.

"If we are found dead it will NEVER be because we committed suicide. It will be cold blooded murder, just as they did at Ruby Ridge, The World Trade Center, Waco, and Oklahoma City."
William Cooper

Isaiah Chapter 8, Verse 12: "Do not call conspiracy all that this people call conspiracy, and do not fear what they fear, nor be in dread."

2.
Cooper According To Cooper

According to the Website: (www.williamcooper.com), William Cooper was reared in an Air Force family. As a child he lived in many different countries, graduating from Yamato High School in Japan. Since he has traveled through or lived in many different foreign countries Mr. Cooper has a world view much different than most Americans.

William served with the Strategic Air Command, United States Air Force. He held a secret clearance working on B-52 bombers, KC-135 refueling aircraft, and Minuteman missiles. William received his Honorable Discharge from the United States Air Force in 1965.

William joined the United States Navy fulfilling a dream previously frustrated by chronic motion sickness. He served aboard the submarine USS Tiru (SS-416), USS Tombigbee (AOG-11), Naval Support Activity Danang RVN, Naval Security and Intelligence Camp Carter RVN, Danang Harbor Patrol RVN, Dong Ha River Security Group RVN, USS Charles Berry (DE-1035), Headquarters Commander in Chief Pacific Fleet, USS Oriskany (CVA-34).

Cooper was a member of the Office of Naval Security and Intelligence serving as a Harbor and River Patrol Boat Captain at Danang and the Dong Ha River Security Group, Cua Viet, Republic of Vietnam. William Cooper was awarded several medals for his leadership and heroism during combat including two with "V" for Valor.

He served on the Intelligence Briefing Team for the Commander In Chief of the Pacific Fleet. William was the Petty Officer of the Watch and designated KL-47 SPECAT operator in the CINCPACFLT Command Center at Makalapa Hawaii. There he held a Top Secret, Q, SI, security clearance.

William Cooper achieved the rank of First Class Petty Officer, QM1, E-6 after only 8 years of Naval service, a difficult task in any branch of the U.S. military.

William Cooper received an Honorable Discharge from the United States Navy on December 11, 1975.

William attended Long Beach City College where he picked up an Associate of Science Degree in Photography. He founded the Absolute Image Studio and Gallery of Fine Art Photography in Long Beach, California. William held the position of Executive Director of Adelphi Business College, Pacific Coast Technical Institute, and National Technical College. Mr. Cooper was the National Marketing Coordinator for National Education and Software.

ABOVE: Cooper patrolling the Da Nang Harbor

BELOW: Cooper is presented with Naval Commendation
Medal with Combat V

WILLIAM COOPER: DEATH OF A CONSPIRACY SALESMAN

He produced several well-known documentaries covering subjects such as the Kennedy assassination and secret black projects that have built flying disk shaped craft. William is an internationally acclaimed radio personality broadcasting the Hour Of The Time on WBCQ worldwide short-wave 7.415 MHz from 10 PM until 11 PM Eastern Standard Time (0300 to 0400 UTC) Monday through Thursday nights.

William Cooper is the author of Behold A Pale Horse (1991 Light technology Publishing). The book has become the best selling underground book of all time. It is read and promoted by word of mouth by People of all races, religions, and nationalities.

Mr. Cooper is a world class lecturer, one of the few other than superstars, monarchs, and Popes who have appeared at Wembly in London. William Cooper has lectured for 10 years in every State.

William Cooper, Trustee, has founded for Harvest Trust, the CAJI News Service, VERITAS national full size newspaper, The Intelligence Service, Harvest Publications, and has helped over 700 low power FM affiliate stations get equipped and on the air... including the station he managed as Trustee for the Independence Foundation Trust, 101.1 FM Eagar, Arizona, broadcasting to 7,000 people.

Under his leadership Harvest Trust ventured into the publishing trade. The first book under the Harvest Trust imprint was **Oklahoma City: Day One** by Michele Marie Moore... the definitive classic on the Oklahoma City bombing of the Alfred P. Murrah Federal Building on April 19, 1995. Shortly after the bombing, Rush Limbaugh read a White House memo on the air during his broadcast which named William Cooper,"...the most dangerous radio host in America". Mr. Cooper considers William Clinton's pronouncement the greatest compliment that he has ever received.

William Cooper's FBI file, promulgated by the investigation required by his security clearances while in military service, was one of those unlawfully in possession of the White House in what has become known as, "Filegate." Shortly after this discovery President Clinton ordered all federal agencies to begin investigation, persecution, and prosecution of Mr. Cooper to shut him up.

After years of filing FOIA requests and researching the IRS William Cooper brought suit against the IRS in Federal District Court in Phoenix Arizona to force the IRS to produce proof of jurisdiction and delegation of authority which the IRS was unable to do. To short circuit Mr. Cooper's attempt to reveal the true nature of the criminal IRS, and to carry out the orders of the White House, the agency lied to a Grand Jury, not allowing William Cooper to testify, and secured indictments against Mr. Cooper and his wife Annie. This ploy successfully stopped Mr. Cooper from continuing his suit against the criminal IRS for fear of being arrested.

In March of 1999, Cooper William sent his family out of the United States for their security. He lived and worked alone with his two dogs, one rooster, and one chicken.

Those Who Knew Cooper Expected a Violent End

Bill Hamilton ~ Having known Bill Cooper I predicted years ago that his life would end this way. He had a real love for firearms and booze. He had a difficult time distinguishing truth from fantasy. I'm only sorry his good qualities did not predominate in his life.

Back in 1988 when I met John Lear, Bill Cooper was starting to post his expose of MJ-12 and the UFO cover-up. I was beginning to look into the MJ-12 enigma myself at the time and worked with Bill Steinman who wrote the book "UFO Crash at Aztec." Steinman was always one of the first to hear about a new whistleblower and that is how I had heard about Cooper.

I was one of the first ones to sponsor a talk by him and was embarrassed afterward when he made a plea for money. Afterwards, having coffee in the restaurant with Bill and his wife, he told me that he had seen something in official documents on the 1954 Edwards AFB incident with Eisenhower.

I was very interested in this rumor and even went someways in investigating the incident. Bill made the startling claim then (and it was recorded during his talk) that it was Pleidians that landed at Edwards in 1954!

I thought this was most peculiar so a few months later I brought up the subject over the phone and he stated to me that he had never said that Pleidians had landed at Edwards because the docs said Reticulans.

I knew then that he was an inveterate liar and he changed his story at least once a month. He also stunned me by inviting me to go to a gun show with him and buy a type of gun that would "blow a hole in an engine block." I asked him why I would want to do a silly thing like that. His reply was that I should protect myself against the government.

He used to drink heavily and got into a fight at one UFO conference in San Diego with Eric Beckjord. When he eventually changed his story from evil aliens to evil government and lost his growing audience, he faded from the UFO conferences and went to Arizona to spread his militia views.

In his book, ***Behold a Pale Horse*** he says that he thought that I was a friend, but I was just another opportunist. I am sorry he felt that way. I found the bulk of this book to be no more than plagiarized works bound under cover with his name on it. The only part that was his was the first chapters on his story which had long since changed since he wrote the book. Farewell Bill. I hope you rest easily in the afterlife as you sure were ill at ease with life on earth.

"I am fully aware of how obnoxious Bill Cooper was, and was particularly disgusted by his attacks on Don and Vicki Ecker. Cooper did die for what he believed in, however. He just happened to believe in some pretty weird stuff. I really think his ugliness was a reflection of the ugliness he saw around him and he was struggling toward a higher plateau. And like any other police shooting, a call for brains-before-bullets needs to be made, and also a nod toward the interconnectedness of local police and the larger police intelligence world."
Kenn Thomas

"Back when I first met Cooper in 1988 he was telling me he might be killed by the "Secret Government" because of his UFO/alien disclosures. Well had that been the case, it took them long enough. Well here in the USA, when you resist arrest using a firearm...the chances are YOU WILL BE KILLED."
Don Ecker

"Bill Cooper was a kick, he lived in "interesting times," and if you have ever read the ancient Chinese curse "May you live in interesting times," you will understand this. I have no sympathy for any involved in his demise, you pick your sides and make your choices, just as Bill did, and just as each and every one of us will have to do."
JAK

3.
UFOs - MJ12 – AREA 51

For a number of years, Bill Cooper had been writing and speaking about the "Ultimate Conspiracy" - the granddaddy of all conspiracies from which all other conspiracies originate. This "all-encompassing" conspiracy involves such diverse elements ranging from the Illuminati to UFOs.

Cooper has summed up his beliefs on his radio show and on his Veritas News Service website. Cooper believed that the following is fact. He would say that this is not a theory, it is a genuine conspiracy.

I witnessed the Top Secret/Majic documents from which this information is excerpted while a member of the United States Navy attached to the Intelligence Briefing Team of Admiral Bernard Clarey, Commander in Chief of the United States Pacific Fleet.

I certify that the following information is true and correct to the best of my memory and the research that I have accomplished. I will swear to it in any court of Law.

I can produce the names of approximately 38 U.S. Navy officers and enlisted men who witnessed these documents while in the service of their country. I can produce the names of approximately 8 people involved in the UFO deception who have witnessed these documents. I can produce the names of approximately 80 others whom I suspect have witnessed these same documents. I will not reveal the names except in a court of Law that is willing to prosecute the People and organizations involved in the conspiracy to overthrow the government of the United States of America to bring about a socialist totalitarian world government.

For many years I sincerely believed that an extraterrestrial threat existed and that it was the most important driving force behind world events. I was wrong and for that I most deeply and humbly apologize.

Many years ago I had access to a set of documents that I eventually realized was the plan for the destruction of the United States of America and the formation of a socialist totalitarian world government. The plan was contained within a set of Top Secret documents with the title "MAJESTYTWELVE." There was no space between majesty and twelve. The term honored the planned placement of ultimate power in a body of wise men who are destined to rule the world as the disciples of a Messiah front man. This Messiah will serve as a buffer between the wise men and the people. I discovered these documents between 1970 and 1973 while I was a member of the Intelligence Briefing Team of the Commander in Chief of the United States Pacific Fleet.

MAJESTYTWELVE was in a tall thin font style...imagine the title squeezed together between the M and E with all of the letters stretched vertically. The key to access was a Top Secret (Q) (SCI) security clearance with the compartmentalization of "MAJIC" (not magic). I cannot remember the exact font except that it is a tall thin version of San Serif...the exact name escapes me after all these years... but it is a key to access.

The plan outlined the formation of a world totalitarian socialist government. It is to be ruled by a behind-the-scenes council of wise men. A so-called benevolent dictator, will be presented as the Messiah. The Constitution for the United States of America and its Bill of Rights will be scrapped. A parliamentary form of government will take its place. All military forces and individuals are to be disarmed except for an internal police force which will carry only the minimum weapons needed to maintain internal order.

The only military force will be a world police force under the United Nations in sufficient numbers with state-of-the-art technology so that it can field overwhelming force against any perceived threat to the world supra government - see State Department Publication 7277. The military of the United States of America is currently filling the requirement. The senior officer corps of all of our military forces has betrayed their oaths of allegiance to the Constitution and has joined the conspiracy. They are turncoats who are actively engaged in High Treason.

The source of this conspiracy will be found in the body known as the Illuminati. It is made up of the highest adepts of the combined total of the so-called fraternal orders and secret societies. They are bound together by blood oaths, a secret religion, and the promise of an elite status within regional government, or the world supra government.

Their religion is based upon the Kabbalah, the Luciferian Philosophy, and the worship of the Sun. They are not bound by any oath or allegiance save their own. They are loyal to no government or People save their own. And they are Citizens of no country save their already in place secret world government. In their own words, "If you are not one of us you are nothing." To garner some sense of "feel|" for the concept see the movie They Live.

You cannot hope to understand the philosophy (Illuminism) of any branch of the "Mystery School" (Illuminati) without many years of study and a complete knowledge of their "symbolic" language. You must understand that like many other organizations they attract those who completely miss the boat...or are just too stupid to "get it."

19

WILLIAM COOPER: DEATH OF A CONSPIRACY SALESMAN

When an individual joins a branch of the "Brotherhood," by any name, Freemasonry, Theosophical Society, Anthroposophic Society, Fraternitis Rosae Crucae, Knights Templar, Sovereign and Military Order of the Knights of Malta, or any other fraternal order or secret society, no one ever sits down with them and explains the meaning of anything.

An actual literal esoteric education would be too dangerous. It could result in a public expose, something which the Illuminati must avoid at all cost. But to give those who might understand a shortcut - Illuminism is COMMUNISM.

The organization of the "Order" is a pyramidal structure of "Degrees." On the bottom are the so-called "Blue" lodges full of ignorant, materialistic, and opportunistic fools. Promising candidates are chosen to be guided up the ladder of initiation with the help of those who have gone before. The initiate is presented with the objects of study, books, symbols, ritual, and camaraderie... but Illumination must come from within.

Each Degree of initiation provides a new key to ultimate enlightenment, but only for those who can truly understand the ritual and symbols of the Degree. Where understanding or the ability to keep the secrets stops... the progress of the candidate stops. Only those above the 29th Degree have the ability to understand the ultimate secrets and goals of the "Order."

The real power are men who are always recruited without exception from the secret societies of Harvard and Yale known as the Skull & Bones and the Scroll & Key. Both societies are secret branches (also called the Brotherhood of Death) of what is otherwise historically known as the Illuminati. Their goal is to rule the world. The doctrine of this group is not democracy or communism, but is a form of fascism. The doctrine is totalitarian socialism. You must begin to think correctly. The Illuminati are not Communists, but some Communists are Illuminati

The ultimate "secret" is the method of controlling large numbers of fools with the promise of a "secret" which they are led to believe will make them one of the "elect." The goal is the elimination of all religion save theirs, the elimination of all nation states, and complete control and ownership of everything, and everyone, everywhere, every moment of every day.

The following document was released by William Cooper to members of various UFO research and patriot research. The manuscript, which ties together certain aspects of the "Secret Government" and the UFO Phenomena, was titled: THE SECRET GOVERNMENT (The Origin, Identity, and Purpose of MJ-12. May 23, 1989. Updated November 21, 1990):

Cooper would later change his mind on the validity of this document, saying that UFOs were part of a massive New World Order disinformation campaign designed to convince the world that evil extraterrestrials threatened the planet.

I originally wrote this piece as a research paper. It was first delivered at the MUFON Symposium on July 2, 1989, in Las Vegas, Nevada. Most of this knowledge comes directly from, or as a result of my own research into the TOP SECRET/MAJIC material which I saw and read between the years 1970 and 1973 as a member of the Intelligence Briefing Team of the Commander in Chief of the Pacific Fleet.

Since some of this information was derived from sources that I cannot divulge for obvious reasons, and from published sources which I cannot vouch for... (this) must be termed a hypothesis. I firmly believe that if the aliens are real, THIS IS THE TRUE NATURE OF THE BEAST. It is the only scenario that answers all the questions and places the various fundamental mysteries in an arena that makes sense.

It is the only explanation which shows the chronology of events and demonstrates that the chronologies, when assembled, match perfectly. The bulk of this I believe to be true if the material that I viewed in the Navy is authentic. As for the rest, I do not know, and that is why this paper must be termed a hypothesis. Most historic and current available evidence supports this hypothesis.

During the years following World War II the government of the United States was confronted with a series of events which were to change beyond prediction its future and with it the future of humanity. These events were so incredible that they defied belief. A stunned President Truman and his top military commanders found themselves virtually impotent after having just won the most devastating and costly war in history. However, now they were faced with the possibility that the human race was not alone in the universe.

The United States had developed, used, and was the only nation on earth in possession of the atomic bomb. This new weapon had the potential to destroy an enemy, and even the Earth itself. At that time the United States had the best economy; the most advanced technology, the highest standard of living, exerted the most influence, and fielded the largest and most powerful military forces in history.

We can only imagine the confusion and concern when the informed elite of the United States Government discovered that an alien spacecraft piloted by 'insect-like' beings from a totally incomprehensible culture had crashed in the desert of New Mexico. Between January 1947 and December 1952 at least 16 crashed or downed alien craft, 65 bodies, and one live alien were recovered. An additional alien craft had exploded and nothing was recovered from that incident. Of these events, 13 occurred within the borders of the United States, not including the craft which disintegrated in the air. Of these 13, one was in Arizona, 11 were in New Mexico, and one was in Nevada. Sightings of UFOs were so numerous that serious investigations and debunking of each report became impossible, utilizing the existing intelligence assets.

An alien craft was found on February 13, 1948, on a mesa near Aztec, New Mexico. Another craft was located on March 25, 1948, in White Sands Proving Ground. It was 100 feet in diameter. A total of 17 alien bodies were recovered from those two crafts. Of even greater significance was the discovery of a large number of human body parts stored within both of these vehicles. A demon had reared its head and paranoia quickly took hold of everyone in the know. The Secret lid immediately became a Top Secret lid and was screwed down tight. The security blanket was even tighter that imposed upon the Manhattan Project. In the coming years these events were to become the most closely guarded secrets in the history of the world.

A special group of America's top scientists were organized under the name Project SIGN in December 1947 to study the phenomena. The whole nasty business was contained. Project SIGN evolved into Project GRUDGE in December 1948. A low-level collection and disinformation project named BLUE BOOK was formed under GRUDGE. Sixteen volumes were to come out of GRUDGE. "Blue Teams" were put together to recover the crashed disks or live aliens. The Blue Teams were later to evolve into Alpha Teams under Project POUNCE.

During these early years the U.S. Air Force and the CIA exercised complete control over the "Alien Secret." In fact, the CIA was formed by Presidential Executive Order first as the Central Intelligence Group for the express purpose of dealing with the alien presence. Later the National Security Act was passed, establishing it as the Central Intelligence Agency. The National Security Council was established to oversee the intelligence community and especially the alien endeavor. A series of National Security Council memos and Executive orders removed the CIA from the sole task of gathering foreign intelligence and slowly but thoroughly legalized direct action in the form of covert activities at home and abroad.

On December 9, 1947, Truman approved issuance of NSC-4, entitled: Coordination of Foreign Intelligence Information Measures, at the urging of the Secretaries Marshall, Forrestal, Patterson, and the director of the State Department's Policy Planning Staff, George Kennan.

The Foreign and Military Intelligence Book One, Final Report of the Select Committee to Study Governmental Operations with Respect to Intelligence Activities, United States Senate, 94th Congress, 2nd Session, Report No. 94-

755, April 26, 1976, p. 49. states, "This directive empowered the Secretary to coordinate oversees information activities designed to counter communism."

A Top Secret annex to NSC-4, NSC-4 A, instructed the director of Central Intelligence to undertake covert psychological activities in pursuit of the aims set forth in NSC- 4. The initial authority given the CIA for covert operations under NSC-4A did not establish formal procedures for either coordinating or approving these operations. It simply directed the DCI to "undertake covert actions and to ensure, through liaison with Senate and Defense, that the resulting operations were consistent with American policy."

Later NSC-10/1 and NSC-10/2 were to supersede NSC-4 and NSC-4 A and expand the covert abilities even further. The Office of Policy Coordination (OPC) was chartered to carry out an expanded program of covert activities. NSC-10/1 and NSC-10/2 validated illegal and extralegal practices and procedures as being agreeable to the national security leadership. The reaction was swift. In the eyes of the intelligence community "no holds were barred."

Under NSC-10/1 an Executive Coordination Group was established to review, but not approve, covert project proposals. The ECG was secretly tasked to coordinate the alien projects. NSC-10/1 & /2 were interpreted to mean that no one at the top wanted to know about anything until it was over and successful.

These actions established a buffer between the President and the information. It was intended that this buffer serve as a means for the President to deny knowledge if leaks divulged the true state of affairs. This buffer was used in later years for the purpose of effectively isolating succeeding Presidents from any knowledge of the alien presence other than what the secret government and the intelligence community wanted them to know. NSC-10/2 established a study panel which met secretly and was made up of the scientific minds of the day. The study panel was not called MJ-12. Another NSC memo, NSC-10/5 further outlined the duties of the study panel. These NSC memos and secret executive orders set the stage for the creation of MJ-12 only four years later.

The live alien that had been found wandering in the desert from the 1949 Roswell crash was named EBE. The name had been suggested by Dr. Vannevar Bush and was short for Extraterrestrial Biological Entity. EBE had a tendency to lie, and for over a year would give only the desired answer to questions asked. Those questions which would have resulted in an undesirable answer went unanswered. At one point during the second year of captivity he began to open up. The information derived from EBE was startling, to say the least. This compilation of his revelations became the foundation of what would later be called the "Yellow Book." Photographs were taken of EBE which, among others, I was to view years later in Project Grudge.

In late 1951 EBE became ill. Medical personnel had been unable to determine the cause of EBE's illness and had no background from which to draw... Several experts were called in to study the illness. These specialists included medical doctors, botanists, and entomologists. A botanist, Dr. Guillermo Mendoza, was brought in to try and help him recover. Dr. Mendoza worked to save EBE until June 2, 1952, when EBE died. Dr. Mendoza became the expert on at least this type of alien biology. The movie E.T. is the thinly disguised story of EBE.

In a futile attempt to save EBE and to gain favor with this technologically superior race, the United States began broadcasting a call for help early in 1952 into the vast regions of space. The call went unanswered but the project, dubbed SIGMA, continued as an effort of good faith.

President Truman created the supersecret National Security Agency (NSA) by secret Executive order on November 4, 1952. Its primary purpose was to decipher the alien communications, language, and establish a dialogue with the extraterrestrials. The most urgent task was a continuation of the earlier effort. The secondary purpose of the NSA was to monitor all communications and emissions from any and all electronic devices worldwide for the purpose of gathering intelligence, both human and alien, and to contain the secret of the alien presence. Project SIGMA was successful. The NSA also maintains communications with the secret Luna base and other secret space programs.

By executive order of the President, the NSA is exempt from all laws which do not specifically name the NSA in the text of the law as being subject to that law. That means that if the agency is not spelled out in the text on any and every law passed by the Congress it is not subject to that or those laws. The NSA now performs many other duties and in fact is the premier agency within the intelligence network. Today the NSA receives approximately 75 per cent of the monies allotted to the intelligence community. The old saying "where the money goes therein the power resides" is true. The DCI today is a figurehead maintained as a public ruse. The primary task of the NSA is still alien communications, but now includes other extraterrestrial projects as well.

President Truman had been keeping our allies, including the Soviet Union, informed of the developing alien problem. This had been done in case the aliens turned out to be a threat to the human race. Plans were formulated to defend the Earth in case of invasion. Great difficulty was encountered in maintaining international secrecy. It was decided that an outside group was necessary to coordinate and control international efforts in order to hide the secret from the normal scrutiny of governments by the press. The result was the formation of a secret ruling body which became known as the Bilderberger Group. The group was formed and met for the first time in 1952. They were named after the first publicly known meeting place, the Bilderberg Hotel. That public meeting took place in 1954. They were nicknamed the Bilderbergers. The headquarters of this group is Geneva, Switzerland. The Bilderbergers evolved into a secret world government that now controls everything. The United Nations was then, and is now, an international joke.

~ PRESS RELEASE ~
"Area-51 Still Active"... Popular Mechanics Article Was Government Propaganda. Dateline - VERITAS News Service - by William Cooper For Immediate Release September 1, 1997

The Harvest Trust expedition to the Tickaboo Valley over the Labor Day weekend witnessed the testing of super-secret technology over Area-51 . The base has not moved nor has testing been shifted to any other site. The *Popular Mechanics* article written by Jim Wilson, Science/Technology Editor, seems to have been an intentional act of propaganda designed to stem the flow of the curious adventure seekers who hope to get a glimpse of the advanced aviation technology being tested at this top-secret remote desert site.

Observation of the 2 known entrances to Groom Dry Lake demonstrated no reduction of traffic from previous years. The Tickaboo Valley entrance was busy with the normal bus load of workers entering the site in the morning and leaving in the late afternoon. Automobile and security vehicles drove in and out on a regular basis. The camo-clad security details in their 4-wheel drive blazers blanketed the area. A couple of large 18 wheeler trucks were observed entering via the entrance south of Rachel in Sand Springs Valley. Both entrances were open...there are no gates or chains on either entrance. Jim Wilson's photo of the chained and locked gate to "Area-51" that appeared in *Popular Mechanics* magazine is an intentional deception.

There is no fence, gate, or chain at the Tickaboo Valley entrance to the test site. These are the signs on the left side of the road at the entrance. There is another set on the right. We observed aircraft and helicopters flying in and out of the site as well as above the site on numerous occasions over the weekend. We observed testing of the saucer only on Sunday night August 31st. The craft ascended over a high mountain peak just north of the Groom Lake facility at approximately 11 PM PDT.

The testing is now apparently being conducted in the valley between the highest mountain peaks to the north of the dry lake bed in an effort to escape detection by those watching outside the boundary of Area-51. On four occasions the craft rose far enough above the peak for us to get a good view of the machine and its unconventional maneuvers.

The vehicle being tested was a huge orange glowing saucer shaped machine that hovered, ascended, descended and made sharp right angle turns as well as very fast circular spinning maneuvers that are impossible utilizing conventional aircraft. All those in our party were able to make very good observations using binoculars and spotting scopes. Some photographs were taken.

The technology is not "alien" except in the sense that the prototype may have been developed by the Germans during WW-II. The technology that flies above Area-51 belongs to the United States of America. It is operated either from remote control or is piloted by humans. It is far superior to anything the public has ever known.

We were constantly watched by the armed security patrols in 4-wheel drive vehicles. We were always covered by at least 3 and a maximum of 5 security teams at all times day and night. When we went to the entrance to the test site in the Tickaboo Valley a security team observed us from the top of the hill directly south of the entrance. Six ominous signs lined the sides of the road. The most chilling stated, "Use of Deadly Force Authorized."

Behold A Pale Horse, By Milton William Cooper
1991, Light Technology Publishing, Sedona, Arizona

4.

Bill Cooper: Trouble With The Feds - By Commander X
(Originally Published in *Covert Action*, Issue 3, 1998)

This could almost be expected to happen. Bill Cooper was among the first to "blow the whistle" on the Secret Government. Almost a decade ago, he released information that while he was in Naval Intelligence, he had seen certain papers and documents purporting to establish the fact that not only did the U.S. have proof that ETs existed, but that someone in the early 1950s, had established a treaty with those little buggers known as the grays to swap alien technology for the abduction of humans for cloning and other forms of experimentation.

Cooper spoke widely at seminars and conferences fora a time before he was "silenced" (perhaps by his own doing). Among his assertions: that the Secret Service agent who had been driving the Kennedy limo in Dallas was responsible for the president's assassination.

Hard pressed to prove such allegations (and changing his mind several times), Cooper made his other findings a little more difficult for followers to believe, and now, it turns out that Cooper is in trouble with the Feds.

Middle-of-the-road UFOlogist Jim Moseley tells the story best in a recent issue of Saucer Smear, a neo-radical flying saucer newsletter, from which we quote:

"A front page story in the July 3, 1998 issue of the *Arizona Republic* newspaper informs us that former UFOlogist Bill Cooper is in a showdown with federal authorities in regards to tax evasion. The headline reads "Militiaman Refuses to Recognize Warrant." It seems that Cooper failed to appear in federal court on charges that he evaded income taxes from 1992 to 1994 and defrauded a bank.

"We met Cooper several times at Tim Beckley's western conventions in the early '90s, and we spent some enjoyable interludes drinking with him at hotel bars. On one occasion, Bill was with his oriental wife, Annie Mordhorst, and their young daughter. Cooper made no secret about his disdain for the income tax laws.

"In fact, he and Beckley eventually had a falling out over the mere fact that Beckley mailed him a form regarding the tax liability on the money he (Cooper) earned from his lectures at those conventions - all of which were very well attended, because Cooper is an excellent speaker, whether one agrees with him or not.

WILLIAM COOPER: DEATH OF A CONSPIRACY SALESMAN

"Bill Cooper does not describe himself as a militiaman, but there is no doubt that he is very sympathetic to this extreme right-wing and sometimes violent movement. In regard to the present crisis, Cooper has posted on his Internet site, in big red letters: 'Warning!! Any attempt by the federal government or anyone else to execute the unconstitutional and unlawful arrest warrants issued by Judge Irwin on William and Annie Cooper will be met with armed resistance. Any person who attempts to kidnap our children will be shot upon discovery.'

"Federal agents, fearful of another Ruby Ridge or Waco-type incident, seem to be in no hurry to move in on Cooper. They know where he lives and will move cautiously, but added, 'Obviously at some point we will effect the arrest.' We have seen no follow-up on this front page article.

"Cooper's UFO views are of interest. As a former Navel Intelligence officer, he claims to have seen highly classified documents proving that the U.S. government has captured saucers, interacted with the aliens, etc. However, at a given point in time he reversed his course and decided that these documents were simply disinformation, to make us believe the aliens are here, possible to soften us up for the dreaded forthcoming New World Order.

"Bill Cooper is the author of a book called *Behold A Pale Horse*, which sold quite well a few years ago. We never actually read it, but we did find the page where he lists us as a CIA agent, along with several other UFOlogists. Cooper later told us that he has changed his mind about this too.

"Cooper has a regular radio show on the Christian Broadcasting Network, and your editor once did an hour-long interview on this program which is apparently heard mainly in Europe. Cooper is also the editor of an occasionally-published newspaper called Veritas (Latin for truth). Right-wing views abound in all of this, but we never heard Cooper call for armed resistance to the government except when personally attacked, as Cooper now feels has happened to him.

"Cooper says that no one becomes popular by telling people the truth. History records what happened to the true prophets of the past. However, some have listened to their warnings and were not caught off-guard. Others have put their heads in the sand and refused to listen. In short, we have here a very bright, but strange man with a terrible temper. All in all, we liked him, though we never subscribed to his views on UFOs, politics or anything else."

Cooper Family Targeted by Feds

Anyone who ever dealt with Bill Cooper would always be left with a definite opinion of the man. His strong convictions and abrasive personality irritated even his closest friends, and those who were not experienced with dealing with the man could be left befuddled and angry by the encounter.

In recent years, Cooper had become increasingly belligerent and confrontational with anyone and anything that he perceived represented the sham-government. He refused to pay taxes and threatened people with his ever-present pistol. Finally, federal arrest warrants were issued for him and his wife. In 1998, Cooper published what essentially was a manifesto on the unconstitutionality of the IRS. In this, Cooper publicly warned that any attempts by the government to execute the arrest warrants would be met with armed resistance. The writing was already on the wall.

(Posted on www.williamcooper.com) **WARNING!!** Any attempt by the federal government or anyone else to execute the unconstitutional and unlawful arrest warrants issued by Judge Irwin on William and Annie Cooper will be met with armed resistance. Any person who attempts to kidnap our children will be shot upon discovery.

Judicial notice is hereby served by affiants upon the United States any other interested party named within. This public notice will be construed to comply with provisions necessary to establish presumed fact under the Federal Rules of Civil Procedure and attending State rules should interested parties fail to rebut any given allegation or matter of law addressed herein. The position will be construed as adequate to meet requirements of judicial notice, thus preserving fundamental law. Matters addressed herein, if not rebutted, will be construed to have general application.

This public notice includes all information which will be found by following the links on this page and by following the links found on any page that is linked from this page. A true and correct copy of this Public Notice is on file with and available for inspection at the office of VERITAS national newspaper and at the office of Harvest Trust. This public notice addresses federal jurisdiction, federal authority, jurisdiction and authority of federal agents, the constitutionality and lawful character of the income tax and the Internal Revenue Service, and other agencies of the United States government including but not limited to the Department of the Treasury, and legal application of the Internal Revenue Code.

Any statements or claims made by the Affiants in this public notice, properly rebutted by facts of Law, or by overriding Constitution for the United States of America, Article Three, Supreme Court rulings, shall not prejudice the Lawful validity of other claims not properly rebutted or invalidated by facts of Law.

Bill Cooper, Annie Cooper, and Daughter in Hawaii
Photo Courtesy Sherry Hansen Steiger

WILLIAM COOPER: DEATH OF A CONSPIRACY SALESMAN

This public notice has been published on this website for more than three days which fulfills the legal requirement under the law in accordance to Federal Rules of Civil Procedure and attending rules of the State of Arizona. This public notice is mirrored on three websites in addition to this website.

New Public Notice #3 posted July 6, 1998

On July 2, 1998 Special Agent Steve Fillerup of the Federal Bureau of Investigation approached the bottom of the hill and honked his horn. He attempted to entice us to accept a document that he held in his hand. We refused the document and refused to enter into discussion with him. I told him he was out of his jurisdiction and cited the documentation and Supreme Court cases to that effect which we have in our possession. I told him to inform his traitor supervisors that, "Tell them they stepped on their dicks this time." Special Agent Fillerup replied, "I think we probably did." He got back in his blazer and drove away.

On July 1, 1998, U. S. District Court Judge Irwin (ADL) unconstitutionally and unlawfully stepped outside the jurisdiction and authority of the United States when he issued a bench warrant for the arrest of William and Annie Cooper for not appearing in "his" court on an unconstitutional and unlawful summons which was NEVER served. The United States has no jurisdiction or venue within the territorial boundaries of the State of Arizona except over land that was ceded to the United States by the by the State Legislature.

WARNING!!

Any attempt by the federal government or anyone else to execute the unconstitutional and unlawful arrest warrants issued by Judge Irwin will be met with armed resistance. Any person who attempts to kidnap our children will be shot upon discovery.

We are formed as the constitutional and lawful unorganized Militia of the State of Arizona and the United States of America and have made many public statements to that affect since 1990. All of these statements are on record on tapes of our lectures and broadcasts. These tapes are dispersed in the hands of Americans across the nation. By invading the Sovereign jurisdiction of the State of Arizona to attack the Citizens of the State of Arizona the United States has declared war upon the Citizens of the several States of the Union

Therefore a STATE OF WAR exists between the Citizens of the Union States and the corporate United States.

WILLIAM COOPER: DEATH OF A CONSPIRACY SALESMAN

We will be Free under Constitutional Republican government guaranteed to us by the organic Constitution for the United States of America or we will be dead. This is the land of the free and the home of the brave. We have drawn our line in the sand.

State and Federal Militia Law

Sources within local "policing agencies" have informed us that the Federal Bureau of Investigation has been put on notice by several ranking local law enforcement personnel that, "We will absolutely not allow another 'Ruby Ridge' or 'Waco' to occur in Apache County, Arizona." Glenn Jacobs, owner and publisher of the Round Valley Paper, spoke personally last night to the Apache County Sheriff. The Sheriff told Glenn, "I have put the FBI on notice that they are not welcome to come into this County and harass the Cooper family."

It appears that we, William and Annie Cooper, have been targeted for imprisonment or extermination by the federal government and the Anti Defamation League (ADL) for documenting and sourcing the truth about the tyranny and despotism of the Illuminati's coming socialist totalitarian new world order. We have worked feverishly since 1988 documenting and sourcing the facts of the treason being brought about by the Illuminati's socialist change agents in government, and through the activities of Secret Societies and organizations such as the subversive Anti Defamation League. They picked on the wrong People. We are not criminals. Everything we have ever done has been in good faith and with reasonable cause. We are not afraid. We will not run and hide. We will continue to oppose evil whenever and wherever we find it. We will stand and fight whomever or whatever assault they may mount against us.

I first learned of the treason taking place in this country (and around the world) when I discovered the plan named "MAJESTYTWELVE" while a member of the Intelligence Briefing Team and Petty officer of the watch in the command center of Admiral Bernard Clarey who at that time was the Commander in Chief of the Pacific Fleet.

The plan outlined the implementation of all of the planks of the Communist Manifesto which began with the graduated so-called Income Tax administered by the fiction known as the Internal Revenue Service, the disarmament of the American People through laws instigated by a series of "terrorist" acts, the formation of a world police force made up of the United Nations force known as NATO combined with the military forces of the United States and the members of the United Nations force known as the

WILLIAM COOPER: DEATH OF A CONSPIRACY SALESMAN

"Warsaw Pact" which plan is outlined in State Department Publication 7277. It documented the intent to demonize and target Patriots and so-called "tax protestors" through "Project Trojan Horse"... and more.

We have been documenting and sourcing the facts of this plan since 1988 through my book Behold A Pale Horse, my radio broadcast Hour Of The Time, in our full size national newspaper VERITAS, Oklahoma City: Day One, and in lectures and speaking engagements throughout the nation and the world. I have made over 150 predictions of coming major world events since 1988 based upon the above information supplemented by many years of research and have only been wrong once.

The Illuminati socialist President of the United States of America, William Jefferson Clinton, wrote in a White House memo that, "William Cooper is the most dangerous radio host in America." The Illuminati's Rush Limbaugh read the memo on his so-called Excellence In Broadcasting Network in 1995 following the bombing of the Alfred P. Murrah Federal Building in Oklahoma City, Oklahoma in an cowardly effort to redirect the socialist attack on so-called "right wing" radio hosts away from himself and onto me while touting himself as "the most dangerous radio host in America."

My FBI record, which was initiated by the investigation required by my Secret security clearance while in the U.S. Air Force, and my Top Secret Q (SI) security clearance while in the U.S. Navy, was one of those found in possession of the White House during the scandal known as "Filegate." President Clinton ordered that all agencies of government begin an investigation naming us enemies of the administration and "domestic terrorists." Since when is telling the truth terrorism in this country?

After 14 issues of VERITAS which exposed, documented, and sourced the facts of the treason and the fraud of the so-called income tax administered by the so-called IRS, a series of 8 broadcasts exposing the Anti Defamation League as a criminal and subversive organization, our publication of the scathing expose Oklahoma City: Day One by Michele Marie Moore, and the most recent results of our extensive OKC bombing investigation, the government and the ADL ordered their puppets to go after us with the intent of shutting us up for good.

U.S. Attorney Janet Reno, the butcher of Waco, ordered the Nazi Gestapo to go after us which immediately launched investigations by the FBI, IRS, Financial Crimes Network, and many others. Reno also ordered her Phoenix based puppet U.S. Attorney Janet Napolitano to shut us up. Our investigation demonstrates that Janet Reno, Phoenix based United States Attorney Janet Napolitano, Assistant United States Attorney Winerip and Special Agent Frank Shupnik, and possibly Judge Irwin are members of the ADL. Shupnik and Winrip have been the most persistent and subversive of the Law in their relentless persecution of this family.

Since my Honorable Discharge from the United States Navy on December 11, 1975, 1 have engaged myself in research to discover if the information regarding the federal income tax that I had seen in MAJESTYTWELVE could be documented. Of all the subjects that I have researched over the years, the unconstitutionality and unlawful application of the federal income tax, by the bogus and unconstitutional Internal Revenue Service, to People domiciled within the territorial boundaries of the union states, outside of the constitutional and lawful jurisdiction and authority of the United States government turned out to be the easiest to document and source.

I immediately understood that the income tax is "private law" fraudulently and unconstitutionally applied to the Citizens of the States of the union and others. This becomes obvious when you begin to understand that "tax courts" are not authorized in the Constitution and so must be extrajudicial private courts. Citizens of the States of the union are fraudulently brought under the income tax laws through contracts to which they did not wittingly or willingly subscribe. Any contract where full disclosure of all terms of the contract has not been made to all parties thereto are frauds and are null and void upon their inception but most certainly upon discovery of the fraud.

We demand that the Internal Revenue Service disclose any and all agreements, contracts, adhesions, laws, regulations, or statutes which make us liable to file and/or pay the so-called income tax. We demand the Internal Revenue Service disclose the true nature of the legal fiction which the IRS contends is us.

When the government began its investigation (persecution) of this family we were noticed by Special Agent Frank Shupnik (no summons) to present ourselves and all our financial records at a meeting to be held between him and us in Phoenix, Arizona...we refused. Compulsory Production of Documents: This brief explains the operation of the Fifth Amendment in reference to producing personal books and records to an agency of the government.

We then began a series of Freedom of Information Requests (FOIA) which, along with our and other's legal research, revealed that they had no authority whatsoever to conduct such an investigation. In fact it once again confirmed that the federal government has no authority or federal jurisdiction within the territorial boundaries of any state of the union whatsoever except on property purchased by the government where jurisdiction has been ceded to the federal government by the state's legislature and over only those specific crimes enumerated in the Constitution for the united States of America.

WILLIAM COOPER: DEATH OF A CONSPIRACY SALESMAN

There is only one exception and that is extraterritorial jurisdiction brought about by treaties with foreign nations such as the Crown of England. We are not citizens of any foreign government. We are not subjects of the Crown of England or Great Britain. We are not subjects of the Queen of England or Great Britain. If you think this is far fetched be forewarned that these people are noted in the Internal Revenue Manual as being subject to the Tax.

My research was confirmed with the following:
"The power of the United States to tax is limited to persons, property, and business within their jurisdiction, as much as that of a state is limited to the same subjects within its jurisdiction." - Supreme Court Justice Fields
And then this by the Supreme Court of New York:
The Supreme Court of New York was presented with the issue of whether the State of New York had jurisdiction over a murder committed at Fort Niagara, a federal fort. In People v. Godfrey, 17 Johns. 225, 233 (N.Y. 1819), that court held that the fort was subject to the jurisdiction of the State since the lands therefore had not been ceded to the United States:
"To oust this state of its jurisdiction to support and maintain its laws, and to punish crimes, it must be shown that an offense committed within the acknowledged limits of the state, is clearly and exclusively cognizable by the laws and courts of the United States. In the case already cited, Chief Justice Marshall observed, that to bring the offense within the jurisdiction of the courts of the union, it must have been committed out of the jurisdiction of any state; it is not, the offence committed, but the place in which it is committed, which must be out of the jurisdiction of the state."
The IRS makes it own rules (constitutes unconstitutional legislative action) but the Internal Revenue Manual Handbook. 10.3.1.1 Chap. 7 Enforcement Activities and Investigative Techniques admits no agent of the United States government has any authority or jurisdiction to serve a summons or arrest warrant anywhere other than "within the jurisdiction of the United States":
[10.3.1.1] 7.2.3 (10/01/96) Service and Return
"An arrest warrant can be executed by a federal marshal or by some other officer authorized by law. The summons may be served by any person authorized to serve a summons in a civil action; however, Inspectors should make every effort to serve their own summonses. The arrest warrant can be executed, and the summons served, at any place within the jurisdiction of the United States."
Years ago I discovered that the Internal Revenue Service is NOT an agency of the Department of the Treasury or the federal government. It is not listed as required by law in the United States Code under the organization of

36

the Department of the Treasury nor is the Bureau of Alcohol, Tobacco, and Firearms, or the Secret Service, nor are any of these bogus agencies listed in the United States Code as agencies of any other branch of government. These agencies are in fact fictions.

And then I discovered the reason why. The United States Supreme Court in Brushaber v. Union Pacific Railroad Company while ruling that the income tax is an excise (indirect tax) included as a part of its ruling that the federal income tax is VOID because Congress unconstitutionally delegated legislative power to the Secretary of the Treasury to write the Law concerning the administrative and enforcement procedures. It was a blatant and unconstitutional breach of the separation of powers and in any case the Constitution does not grant Congress the ability to delegate its powers to anyone or anything or any entity. The IRS, BATF, the Secret Service, and all of their administrative rules, regulations, and enforcement powers were created unconstitutionally by the stroke of a pen of a Department of the Treasury employee. That is why there is so much subterfuge and so many lies involved in the administration and enforcement of the tax by the so-called Internal Revenue Service.

Uncertainty of the Law: American courts have failed to identify what is the nature of the income tax. This uncertainty of the constitutional classification of this form of taxation presents a monumental due process problem for the American people. Members of Congress should be informed of this uncertainty of the law which they did not create.

On January 8, 1991, the U.S. Supreme Court ruled that Americans who refuse to pay their income taxes because they sincerely believe that the tax law is unconstitutional COULD NOT be convicted of willful tax evasion! According to Justice Byron White "someone's good faith belief that a federal tax on his or her wages is unlawful, would not make that person guilty of a crime requiring willful action, no matter how unreasonable that persons belief."

Even if the income tax were constitutional it is misapplied to the Citizens of the States of the union except where the IRS can prove that a Citizen has contracted, with full disclosure by the IRS to that Citizen of all terms and liabilities of that contract, to make him or herself liable. American Legacy Resources wrote one of the best explanations of what the income tax is and what it is not. Visit their Taxation Supplement for a mind expanding experience. Another extremely educational site is called Taxgate. Once you begin to understand how badly you have been defrauded, cheated, and extorted you will never be able to return to sheopledom.

WILLIAM COOPER: DEATH OF A CONSPIRACY SALESMAN

Using our Rights guaranteed by Article One of the first ten amendments known as the "Bill Of Rights" to Free Speech and Freedom of the Press we published several stories revealing the results of our research into the history of, and the Law concerning, the IRS. We also published a lawful "Public Notice" in issues #14, 15, and 16 of VERITAS national newspaper which enumerated certain facts discovered in Dan Meador's and my research. Another "Public Notice" will be published in issues #18, 19, and 20. The law allows us to presume the content of the Public Notice to be "presumed facts" since neither IRS nor the United States government has ever denied any of the facts thus presented.

In light of the above we filed FOIA requests asking the IRS for specific documents which specifically require us to file and pay the so-called income tax... they could not and did not produce any such documentation but sent me a copy of an old 1040 which I had filed before I finally mustered the guts to stop filing based upon the information I had seen in MAJESTYTWELVE and from my research which verified that the tax is a criminal fraud.

The implication was that the 1040s which I had filed in the past was their only authority. In other words I had signed the form stating that I was a "taxpayer." The interpretation of the IRS was that since I had filed previously it was an admission that I was required to file. Hitler would have loved their reasoning. When we filed we filed either by honest mistake because we had not yet discovered the fraud or because of fear and intimidation which is called extortion. Fraud and extortion are criminal acts under the law. When we discovered the fraud we declared all contracts and signatures past, present, and future, which might make us liable to the fraud to be null and void due to fraud.

We also filed FOIA requests asking the IRS for specific documents which gave the IRS the authority to conduct an investigation of a Citizen of Arizona. The IRS could not, and did not, produce any such documentation. We noticed Special Agent Shupnik and Assistant U.S. Attorney Winerip to produce their credentials and documentation of their authority to conduct such an investigation...they refused because no such documents exists.

We learned of an secret agreement between the individual states of the union and the IRS. We obtained an unredacted copy and found that it is an agreement granting jurisdiction to the IRS to require federal employees who are state Citizens and residents of the states to file and pay the so-called federal income tax. No cession of jurisdiction over these people was granted by the state legislature as required by Law. If the so-called Internal Revenue Service has the jurisdiction and authority to require Citizens and residents of the states to file and pay the so-called income tax why do they have to have an special secret agreement between the IRS and the states to tax their federal employees who live and work outside the jurisdiction and authority of the United States government?

We filed suit against the United States government, the IRS, Attorney General Janet Reno, U.S. Attorney for the District of Arizona Janet Napolitano, and others, demanding the court simply order the defendants to either produce the documentation that allows the IRS to tax and/or investigate a Citizen of any state of the union or admit that no such documentation exists, and several other points of Law. The suit has been active for almost three years and the federal judge has refused to order the defendants to obey the law and produce their authority or admit that it does not exist. The attorney for defendants, Katz (another ADL accomplice) has slipped up and admitted in documents that he/she filed in this case that no such documentation (thus no such authority) exists in the Phoenix District. This suit is still awaiting adjudication in United States District Court in Phoenix, Arizona. The government and the ADL wants us in prison or dead before the judge is forced to rule in our favor as he must if he obeys the Law. Recent experience tells us that the courts have been corrupted and the law is frequently ignored. Pro Se litigants are all but ignored by federal judges who pass the cases to clerks to handle.

We were indicted and warrants were issued because we had them against the wall where they could not produce any document giving jurisdiction to the IRS or the federal government. We were targeted and when we were beating them we were indicted.

Later, upon discovery that U.S. District Court in Phoenix is an Article I Court we withdrew our suit against defendants for the reason that Title I Courts have no jurisdiction over Citizens of the Union States. Only Article III Courts and the U.S. Supreme Court have jurisdiction in cases concerning Citizens of Union States. We cannot find an Article III Court existing anywhere in the United States of America. We could not continue our suit anyway since to appear in federal court would result in our arrest.

We have not committed any crime; but on June 18, 1998 a United States Marshall came to the Trust Headquarters in Eagar, Arizona to serve a summons for criminal trial in U.S.

District Court in Phoenix Arizona (or was it federal Tax Court) on "legal fictions" to appear before a Judge Irwin. We told him that we are not the legal fictions named in the summons and ordered him off the Trust property. I told him he was trespassing and that he had no federal jurisdiction or authority within the territorial boundaries of the state of Arizona. He knew I was right and obeyed me without serving the papers. If he had authority and/or jurisdiction why did he not serve the papers and why did he obey my order that he get off Trust property immediately?

Since no legal fictions can be found at our Trust Headquarters and domicile and since no service was made the Court can take no action if Judge Irwin obeys the Law. As we discovered with Waco, Ruby Ridge, and other federal atrocities the federal Courts seldom if ever obey the Law... they just make it up as they go along. The Marshall told me that if the legal fictions named in the summons did not appear in federal Court (or federal Tax Court) in Phoenix, Arizona on July 1, 1998 Judge Irwin would issue a warrant for OUR arrest. We will not appear as we are not the legal fictions named in the summons, the Court has no jurisdiction or authority over us as Citizens of Arizona, and we will not allow an unconstitutional arrest to occur. We will stand and fight their Gestapo with all the means at our disposal any assault which may be mounted upon our property or upon us.

Since the government has created a fictional jurisdiction and since that government is a "corporate" entity vs. the lawful constitutional government it is a fiction and can only lawfully deal with "legal fictions" or people who "volunteer" to fall under their fictional jurisdiction. This is most usually done by fraudulently enticing people to enter into contracts (frauds) where they are never told the terms and consequence of the contract, or by extortion and other trickery.

The federal Marshall was yelling at me across the property and I was yelling back at him in a moderate wind. No papers were served. It is possible that I misconstrued Tax Court for U.S. District Court or visa versa. I only know he had a federal summons signed by a Judge Irwin requiring legal fictions, that use names similar to ours, that he mistook as living at our Trust Headquarters, to appear in a federal court before Judge Irwin on July 1, 1998. He clearly stated that should the legal fictions, which he misconstrued to be us, not appear Judge Irwin would issue a warrant for OUR arrest. No federal court that I am aware of schedules cases to be presented on a 4 day holiday such as the 4th of July. The feds have done this in the past in order that the accused was not be able to appear with an attorney on such short notice, it was not covered by the press, and the feds were able to railroad the accused with no due process, objection, or oversight by the sheople who were happily engaged in their holiday revelry.

Our children will remain with us. They are not shields, as our enemies will claim, any more than children have been shields for families which have been attacked by despotism throughout history. Allowing our children to disappear into the immoral and destructive government child care and foster home industry run by the mind controlling bogus Psychology profession only to be abused and sexually assaulted for many years is a fate worse than death, and we simply will not allow such a thing to happen to our precious little girls.

These people are morally bankrupt and in fact are Nazi jack booted thugs of the worst SS Hitler storm trooper type. They have no ethics, morals, or respect for life, property, religion, or the Law. The Nazis were socialists and socialists are Nazis. They are here among us now. Socialists are in complete and absolute control of the government of the United States of America today.

Please remember that we are not anti-government, radical, fundamentalist, crazy, suicidal, criminals, child molesters, bank robbers, child abusers, tax protestors, wife beaters, husband beaters, drug users, drug dealers, drug growers, drug stock-pilers, revolutionaries, subversives, terrorists, white supremacist, racists, anti-Semitic, or any other demonizing label that may be applied.

We do not have illegal weapons, hand grenades, bombs, missiles, tanks, machine guns, anti-tank rockets, anti-aircraft weapons or any other demonized instrument of any type whatsoever. And our Trust Headquarters and domicile is NOT a compound.

We are formed as the constitutional and Lawful unorganized Militia of the State of Arizona and the United States of America and have made many public statements to that affect since 1990. All of these statements are on record on tapes of our lectures and broadcasts. These tapes are dispersed in the hands of Americans across the nation. By invading the Sovereign jurisdiction of the State of Arizona to attack the Citizens of the State of Arizona the United States has declared war upon the Citizens of the several States of the Union

Therefore a STATE OF WAR exists between the Citizens of the Union States and the corporate United States.

We will be free under constitutional Republican government guaranteed to us by the organic Constitution for the United States of America or we will be dead. This is the land of the free and the home of the brave. We have drawn our line in the sand.

"[W]hen the resolution of enslaving America was formed in Great Britain, the British Parliament was advised by an artful man, who was governor of Pennsylvania, 'to disarm the people; that it was the best and most effectual way to enslave them; but that they should not do it openly, but weaken them, and let them sink gradually.' I ask, who are the militia? They consist now of the whole people, except a few public officers." - Virginia's U.S. Constitution ratification convention, 1788

WILLIAM COOPER: DEATH OF A CONSPIRACY SALESMAN

"That the People have a right to keep and bear Arms; that a well regulated Militia, composed of the Body of the People, trained to arms, is the proper, natural, and safe Defense of a free state." - Within Mason's declaration of "the essential and unalienable Rights of the People," later adopted by the Virginia ratification convention, 1788

Samuel Adams, of Massachusetts:
"The said Constitution [shall] be never construed to authorize Congress to infringe the just liberty of the press, or the rights of conscience; or to prevent the people of the United States, who are peaceable citizens, from keeping their own arms." - Massachusetts' U.S. Constitution ratification convention, 1788

William Grayson, of Virginia:
"[A] string of amendments were presented to the lower House; these altogether respected personal liberty." - Letter to Patrick Henry, June 12, 1789, referring to the introduction of what became the Bill of Rights

Richard Henry Lee, of Virginia:
"A militia when properly formed are in fact the people themselves . . . and include all men capable of bearing arms. To preserve liberty it is essential that the whole body of people always possess arms. The mind that aims at a select militia, must be influenced by a truly anti-republican principle." - Additional Letters From *The Federal Farmer*, 1788

James Madison, of Virginia:
The Constitution preserves "the advantage of being armed which Americans possess over the people of almost every other nation. . . (where) the governments are afraid to trust the people with arms." - *The Federalist*, No. 46

Tench Coxe, of Pennsylvania:
"The militia, who are in fact the effective part of the people at large, will render many troops quite unnecessary. They will form a powerful check upon the regular troops, and will generally be sufficient to over-awe them." - An American Citizen, Oct. 21, 1787

"Who are the militia? Are they not ourselves? Congress has no power to disarm the militia. Their swords and every other terrible implement of the soldier are the birthright of an American.... The unlimited power of the sword is not in the hands of either the federal or state governments, but, where I trust in God it will ever remain, in the hands of the people." - *The Pennsylvania Gazette*, Feb. 20, 1788

"As the military forces which must occasionally be raised to defend our country, might pervert their power to the injury of their fellow citizens, the people are confirmed by the next article (of amendment) in their right to keep and bear their private arms." - *Federal Gazette*, June 18, 1789

Noah Webster, of Pennsylvania:
"Before a standing army can rule, the people must be disarmed; as they are in almost every kingdom in Europe. The supreme power in America cannot enforce unjust laws by the sword; because the whole body of the people are armed, and constitute a force superior to any band of regular troops that can be, on any pretense, raised in the United States. A military force, at the command of Congress, can execute no laws, but such as the people perceive to be just and constitutional; for they will possess the power." - *An Examination of The Leading Principles of the Federal Constitution*, Philadelphia, 1787

Alexander Hamilton, of New York:
"[I]f circumstances should at any time oblige the government to form an army of any magnitude, that army can never be formidable to the liberties of the people while there is a large body of citizens, little if at all inferior to them in discipline and the use of arms, who stand ready to defend their rights and those of their fellow citizens." - *The Federalist*, No. 29

Thomas Paine, of Pennsylvania:
"[Arms discourage and keep the invader and plunderer in awe, and preserve order in the world as well as property... Horrid mischief would ensue were the law-abiding deprived of the use of them." - *Thoughts On Defensive War*, 1775

Fisher Ames, of Massachusetts:
"The rights of conscience, of bearing arms, of changing the government, are declared to be inherent in the people." - Letter to F.R. Minoe, June 12, 1789

Elbridge Gerry, of Massachusetts:
"What, sir, is the use of militia? It is to prevent the establishment of a standing army, the bane of liberty. . . Whenever Government means to invade the rights and liberties of the people, they always attempt to destroy the militia, in order to raise a standing army upon its ruins." - Debate, U.S. House of Representatives, August 17, 1789

WILLIAM COOPER: DEATH OF A CONSPIRACY SALESMAN

Patrick Henry, of Virginia:
"Guard with jealous attention the public liberty. Suspect everyone who approaches that jewel." - Virginia's U.S. Constitution ratification convention

We are intelligent law abiding reasonable People who have drawn our line in the sand. Our enemy will attempt to demonize us in order to obtain the public's permission to murder our whole family just as they did the Weaver family and the Branch Davidians at Waco, Texas. I never thought I would hear so-called Christians whose ancestors fled the old world to escape religious persecution say, "The Branch Davidians deserved what they got... they were just a bunch of religious fanatics," but I heard so-called Christians say it over and over and over again. No People should ever be forced to live in the aura of FEAR that permeates this nation today.

If we are found dead it will NEVER be because we committed suicide. It will be cold blooded murder, just as they did at Ruby Ridge, The World Trade Center, Waco, and Oklahoma City.

We are pro-government, lawful government, lawful Constitutional Republican government as guaranteed to us in the Constitution for the United States of America. We know what the government is and what it is not. We know that the Constitution for the united States of America constitutes the lawful government and anything or anyone outside its strictures, limits, and powers is operating unlawfully and are in fact outlaws.

We know that the Constitution was not penned by a bunch of dottering old men who did not understand the complexities of the modern age over two hundred years ago. The Constitution was produced by the greatest collection of geniuses who have ever lived. It is the LIVING Supreme Law of our country. It provides within the document itself the provisions for us to make any changes that we may deem necessary. Only a very few changes (Amendments) have ever been made. Those changes or deletions wished for by the socialist/communist Illuminati have been rejected by the American People. That last fact necessitates the demonization of the Constitution and all who support it.

I have served my government all my life. I have been a member of the United States Air Force and the United States Navy. I am a combat veteran of the Vietnam War. I fought as a River Patrol Boat Captain in Vietnam earning medals with the "V" for Valor. I took an Oath to, "support and defend the Constitution for the United States of America against all enemies foreign and DOMESTIC." I intent to fulfill that Oath until the day I die...and after, if that is possible.

WILLIAM COOPER: DEATH OF A CONSPIRACY SALESMAN

What we have included here is by no means the entirety of our legal position. It is barely the beginning, only a few facts and questions that should get you thinking. We will attempt to include much more through links from our Website.

We hope to win this battle although the odds and history tell us that we won't. If we win then all America wins...if we lose the subversive Illuminati socialists in government and the ADL will LOSE big time. We are not afraid. I have engaged and fought better troops than any of the techno-spoiled brats they can or will ever field against us.

In any case whatever happens we as a family will be Free... and due to the sheer volume of our work that is in public hands we will never be forgotten. It makes me very sad to know that all of you will still be enslaved by tyrants and despotism in a totalitarian socialist new world odor (really stinks)... unless you also draw your line and take your stand to fight the last battle for Liberty and Freedom.

Oh...I almost forgot. If they need a negotiator to resolve the situation (won't happen) send Lieutenant Colonel James "Bo" Gritz... I would love to see him coming up the hill to talk us down. Please...oh please... send Gritz.

Please pray for us and keep coming back to our Website: http://williamcooper.com We will keep it updated adding information, documenting, and sourcing our position within the Law, and the corrupted Illuminati puppets despotic and tyrannical disregard and contempt for the Law. Who knows...you may even become awakened and join the fight for Liberty and Freedom for all People regardless of race, religion, or place of ancestral origin.

We stand united in appealing to the Supreme Judge of the World for the rectitude of our intentions; and, with a firm reliance on the real and present protection of divine Providence, mutually pledge to each other our lives, our fortunes, and our sacred honor. In God we trust.

William Cooper, Annie Cooper, Dorothy Cooper, Allyson Cooper & Company

Bill Cooper Killed By Police
The Round Valley Paper - Tuesday, November 06, 2001

Bill Cooper, militia commander, worldwide broadcaster, disk jockey, acid-commentator on the scene, author and publisher, was shot to death by police officers in an exchange of gunfire at midnight Monday, fulfilling his often-stated wish to go out in a blaze of glory.

WILLIAM COOPER: DEATH OF A CONSPIRACY SALESMAN

Around midnight Monday, local police with a warrant for a couple of aggravated-assault warrants (Bill was certainly guilty) went up in force to Bill Cooper's house, letting on to be teenagers drinking and partying, with the radio turned up loud.

Bill came out of his house and drove over to them, demanding that they get off of his mountain. Two officers jumped Bill in his car. Bill backed it up, shoved one officer out and shot the other one twice in the head with his forty-five, but did not inflict any life-threatening wounds.

Bill ran toward his house, whereupon the entire contingent gave Bill what he had been asking for - his martyrdom. This was not a federal ninja action, nor a rogue-cop riot. Bill had gone over to Dr. Scott Hamblin's house and wagged a gun in his face, and seems to have done the same to another person as well. The officers wisely went prepared, as Bill had broadcast hundreds of times that he would not surrender and would kill anyone who came after him.

From: Glenn Jacobs, friend, enemy, neighbor, unindicted co-conspirator, hateful adversary, collaborator, messenger boy, informer and listener.

William Cooper Update Sierra Times 11-06-01

Details are still sketchy on what caused the Cooper shootout on November 5, 2001, but a fax sent from the Apache County Sheriffs office sheds some more light on the subject. William Cooper was fatally wounded during a late night gunfight. Contrary to what was reported earlier, it was not a SWAT raid, but a simple confrontation between police and Cooper.

One Apache County deputy, Robert Martinez was critically wounded in the exchange. Here's what we know so far:

According to the Sheriffs report, several deputies were positioned outside the Cooper residence to serve a warrant for aggravated assault and two counts of endangerment. Cooper had stated numerous times in the past that he would not surrender to law enforcement via his Website and shortwave radio. Obviously, law enforcement took him seriously. The showdown began at approximately 12:15 PM local time.

After leaving his residence in his vehicle, the report states that Cooper confronted plain clothed deputies a short distance away. "As Cooper drove back to his residence, deputies attempted to stop him using a fully marked patrol vehicle to block the driveway. Cooper refused to stop or comply with verbal orders by the deputies," according to the report.

Cooper then drove around the patrol car to evade the arrest, and the report stated that he tried to run over one of the deputies en route back to his residence. Cooper was then followed a short distance to his residence where this time he was confronted by uniformed deputies. "After refusing once again to comply with the deputies orders, Cooper exited his vehicle and began running toward the house, firing shots with a handgun toward the deputies," the report said. No where in the report did it mention that Cooper only had one leg - the other lost in combat long ago. Cooper died on the scene.

When Deputy Martinez took a head shot, officers returned fire, the report said. According to the Sheriffs office, "the surgery on Martinez went well," but the condition is still critical. There was a positive history written up about Martinez in the report, but nothing positive about Cooper, of course.

Cooper had made it known that he would take action against law enforcement from years back stating, "Trespassers will be shot on discovery." He also denied violating any laws during that period as well. Cooper has a history of harassing and threatening local residents with deadly force, according to the report. He was recently charge with aggravated assault and endangerment, as well as wanted by the U.S. Marshall's Service on unrelated felony charges. Cooper had spent the last month challenging the government's claims about what caused the destruction of the World Trade Center on September 11.

Most who knew of Cooper all state that he was a hard man to get along with - if at all. His demeanor and attitude was "unfriendly" at best. Although state-sponsored media called Cooper a "national militia leader," no one has yet to come forward who was under his command, nor has anyone to this point come forward to claim his 'militia rank.'

None of those who knew Cooper and spoke to Sierra Times wanted to go on the record, but the best statement was, "he was a son-of a bitch, but he was our son-of-a bitch."

The new Patriot Act of 2001 has many wondering if the Cooper take down was just the beginning in silencing the voices on opposition in the Country. "Are they just starting in alphabetical order?" one person asked. Cooper was best known for being the first to provide evidence of explosives being found inside the Murrah Building in Oklahoma City on April 19, 1995, including the type of explosive used.

According to his webmaster, "It appears at this time to be totally unrelated to the disputes he had with the federal government." There were no federal agents involved with the gunfight. According to Detective Frank Valenzuela of the Arizona Department of Public Safety, the shooting took place at 11:40 PM outside of Cooper's home at 96 North Clearview Circle, Eager, AZ.

Det. Valenzuela stated that Deputies from the Apache County Sheriffs Department were attempting to serve an arrest warrant upon Mr. Cooper. The Warrant, issued by the Round Valley Judicial Precinct in Springerville, AZ charged Cooper with one Count of Aggravated Assault With A Deadly Weapon, and two Counts of "Endangerment." The Warrant was issued on August 29,2001 for an incident which allegedly took place on July 11, 2001. The Court Case Number on the Warrant is CR-01-0310. Neither Valenzuela, nor the Apache County Attorney's Office would reveal the name of the alleged victim(s). They did say the complaint was signed by Detective Paul Kirkum of the Eager, AZ Sheriffs Dept. According to Valenzuela, Police had intelligence that Cooper had a large quantity of weapons in his home, and possibly explosives. Valenzuela also said the police knew that during his radio show on WBCQ, Cooper repeatedly stated that he "would kill any law enforcement officers that tried to take him."

Militia Broadcaster Killed By Law Officers - By Mark Shaffer
The Arizona Republic - 11-7-1

EAGER - One of the country's most influential militia radio broadcasters was killed early today in a hail of gunfire when law officers tried to arrest him on a warrant accusing him of aggravated assault.

William Milton Cooper, 58, whose apocalyptic, constitutionalist shortwave radio programs were a major influence on Oklahoma City bomber Timothy McVeigh, was shot to death after Cooper shot and critically wounded an Apache County sheriff's deputy who had tried to arrest him, police said.

The officer, Robert Marinez, 40, was listed in critical condition at St Joseph's Hospital and Medical Center in Phoenix.

Apache County Sheriff Brian Hounshell said Martinez, a former Marine and Persian Gulf War veteran, was shot twice in the head by what was believed to be a .45-caliber pistol.

The officer is expected to survive, Hounshell said, after undergoing two hours of surgery this morning. Marinez's skull was fractured, and surgeons removed bone fragments from near his brain, the sheriff said.

Cooper had been indicted on federal charges of failing to pay taxes from 1992 to 1994 and became a fugitive after failing to appear for a U.S. District Court hearing in Phoenix three years ago.

Scott Garms, Eagar's police chief, said he had urged federal law officers to stay away from Cooper's two-story compound, high on a mesa overlooking Round Valley, because militia group members do not recognize the legitimacy of federal law officers.

"We certainly didn't want to make him a martyr," Garms said.

The police chief said the effort to arrest Cooper became a local law enforcement matter in July after Cooper ordered a local man to leave land that

Cooper did not own atop the mesa and then followed the man about two miles to his home. Cooper then pulled a gun and pointed it at the man's face, Garms said. That resulted in a warrant for Cooper's arrest.

Seventeen officers were involved in the operation, which started at 11:40 p.m. Monday, Garms and Hounshell said.

Garms said a group of undercover officers in a pickup truck pretended to be "people just acting normal up there at night" in a ruse to draw Cooper out of his house to adjoining property 200 yards away. But Cooper surprised the officers by driving, not walking, to them, and he never left the vehicle during a verbal altercation.

During that confrontation, a second undercover police vehicle drove to Cooper's property line and blocked the road, Garms said. But on the way back to his house, Cooper drove off the side of the road and tried to run over sheriff's Sgt. Steve Brown, who dived out of the way, Hounshell said.

Cooper then parked his vehicle in front of his house, and Marinez followed him toward his front door while admonishing him to surrender, Hounshell said. Near the door, Cooper turned and fired an undetermined number of rounds at Marinez, who was wearing a bulletproof vest but no helmet, Hounshell said, adding that officers had not seen Cooper's handgun before he fired it.

At that point, another sheriff's deputy who had been at the side of Cooper's home, approached Cooper and opened fire. Hounshell said he did not know where or how many times Cooper was struck, saying a state Department of Public Safety shooting-review team had been dispatched to the site. Hounshell declined to identify the officer.

Cooper had said numerous times on his radio show, Hour of the Time, and posted on his Web site, that he had been under siege by "Nazi jackbooted thugs." He also had solicited donations for what he said was his fight against the U.S. government, which he said was responsible for the 1995 bombing of the Alfred P. Murrah Federal Building in Oklahoma City.

"He had vowed that he would not be taken alive," said Tom McCombs, a spokesman for the U.S. Marshal's Service in Phoenix.

Garms said Cooper's radio show had been off the air for about a month because of a shortage of money. But in one of his last programs, Garms said, Cooper had accused the federal government of the Sept.11 terrorist attack on the World Trade Center in New York.

Glenn Jacobs, a Round Valley newspaper publisher and friend of Cooper, said he didn't think the police operation was unjustified.

WILLIAM COOPER: DEATH OF A CONSPIRACY SALESMAN

"I think Bill just went nuts. He was looking for martyrdom anyway and swore he would never surrender," Jacobs said. "They had him dead to rights on the aggravated assault."

Jacobs also said that if the sheriff's deputies had allowed Cooper to enter his house, "they would have had a bloodbath on their hands. He kept an AK-47 just inside his front door by a magazine rack.

A spokesman for a group that tracks militias said the shooting wasn't surprising given Cooper's history. In addition to his show, he was known within the militia movement for an influential book called Behold a Pale Horse, in which he wrote about global New World Order elites, UFOs, and top secret government conspiracies.

"For more than 3 1/2 years, he had been holed up in his house in Eagar, threatening to kill police officers and federal agents," said Mark Potok of the Southern Poverty Law Center. "He was talked about as a. guy who talked crazy and made a lot of threats. The reality is that people like him are frequently exceedingly dangerous."

James Nichols, brother of Oklahoma bombing co-defendant Terry Nichols, said during a 1996 court proceeding that McVeigh had been a regular listener of Cooper's programs in the months leading up to the Murrah bombing.

Nelson Udall, an Eagar repairman and friend of Cooper, also said that McVeigh had paid a personal visit to Cooper two months before the bombing, when Cooper was broadcasting his show from his home at the time in St. Johns.

Cooper, who said he served in the Navy in intelligence operations aboard submarines, also was heavily involved in discussions of unidentified flying objects on his radio programs.

* * *

"Apparently, Cooper had gone into town and was waving his gun around. He'd gone off the handle for some reason or something and the local police figured they had to do something before he ended up hurting someone. This I find completely believable. I knew Cooper extremely well. We worked together VERY closely for several years. I saw him at his best, and I saw him at his worst. And I saw his volatility, the times when he was drunk and disorderly, the times when he behaved irresponsibly, all of those ugly things that make up "real life." I also saw him noble and selfless and giving.

"But Bill did have a dark and uncontrollable side. No question about it. This does not mean that he was not a good patriot, or that he did not teach and help a lot of people. I'm sure he did. But to turn this death - which was so needless and for nothing - into a martyrdom, or to say that the feds did it, is unrealistic and irresponsible.

"From all that can be known locally at the scene at this time, the situation was nothing more than Bill out of control in a public place while armed. And if you've ever been around Bill when he is out of control, you'd call the cops, too. Believe me! You would! Bill out of control is dangerous. Bill out of control with his handgun is deadly. That's the truth. Any one who ever knew him closely will absolutely confirm this. In this situation, we'll find that the police acted responsibly, and Bill, for all his good points and bad, died for nothing."

*Michele Marie Moore - Author, **Oklahoma City: Day One***

5.
Sheriff Report on the Shooting of William Cooper

OFFICE OF THE SHERIFF
Brian R. Hounshell, Sheriff - Apache County, Arizona November 6, 2001

On Nov 5, 2001 at 11:40 pm, Apache County Sheriffs deputies attempted to serve an arrest warrant on a known felon, William Milton Cooper, (58 years of age) at his residence located at 96 North Clearview Circle in Eagar AZ. Cooper was considered armed and dangerous. During the execution of this warrant, Cooper was fatally shot by deputies after he shot and struck a sheriffs deputy.

Members of the Apache County Sheriffs Office deployed several deputies in the area adjacent to Cooper's home in an attempt to draw him from his residence to serve an arrest warrant.

After leaving his residence in his vehicle, Cooper confronted plainclothes deputies a short distance away. As Cooper drove back to his residence, Sheriffs deputies attempted to stop him using a fully marked patrol vehicle to block the roadway.

Cooper refused to stop or comply with verbal orders issued by deputies. Cooper drove around the patrol vehicle off the roadway and attempted to run over a sergeant before heading back to his residence. Cooper was followed a short distance to the front of his residence where he was again confronted by uniformed deputies. After refusing once again to comply with orders from deputies, Cooper exited his vehicle and ran toward his house, firing shots from a handgun towards deputies. Deputy Robert Marinez of the Apache County Sheriffs Office was struck in the head by at least one round.

Deputies returned fire striking and fatally wounding Cooper.

Deputy Marinez was transported by ground ambulance to the White Mountain Regional Medical Center and then flown to a Trauma Unit in Phoenix. Deputy Marinez was last reported to be in critical condition.

Deputy Marinez has served as a law enforcement officer for 4 years and was serving as a tactical officer at the time of the shooting. His experience also includes patrol and criminal investigation. Deputy Marinez is 40 years old and has served as a United States Marine during Operation Desert Shield and Desert Storm. Deputy Marinez is married with three children.

Cooper threatened to kill law enforcement personnel and made those threats known through the use of his web site, radio station and personal messages.

WILLIAM COOPER: DEATH OF A CONSPIRACY SALESMAN

Cooper has a history of harassing and threatening local residents with deadly force. He recently was charged with aggravated assault and endangerment. Cooper was also wanted by the United States Marshall's Office for unrelated felony charges.

Following the shooting, the scene was secured by officers from the Eagar Police Department and Apache County Sheriffs Deputies.

The Arizona Department of Public Safety's Special Investigations Unit is conducting a criminal investigation into the shooting at the request of the Eagar Police Dept. and the Apache County Sheriffs Office.

DPS Special Operations Units were called to the scene to clear the residence of any potential hazards that may exist.

For further information contact: Sheriff Brian Hounshell, Apache County Sheriffs Office (928) or (520) 337-4321 - Chief Scott Garms, Eagar Police Department (928) or (520) 333-4127

SECTION TWO

The Ultimate Secret

6.
Los Angeles Lecture

For those of you who don't know, my name is William Cooper, I was raised in a military family. My family, my ancestors, since they came to this country, have been government people. We have served in the military, we have been patriots, we have fought in all the wars, we care about this country and believe in the Constitution of the United States.

We know, as many people don't know, that the Constitution of the United States of America IS the United States of America! And that's why we've always been ready... to do the things needed...to preserve and protect it. When I left home I went into the Air Force, the Strategic Air Command.

As a child I'd heard stories from my father and pilots, other pilots, my father was a pilot, about Foo Fighters, UFO's, strange craft that were not made on this Earth. And as a kid, you hear that in passing, and it's neat, and you giggle about it, and you go out and play "Space Man," and you forget it.

When I was in the Air Force I met men who had participated in alien crashed-craft recoveries. Now this intrigued me, it interested me, but it was usually after quite a few bottles of beer that these stories would come out, and sometimes the next morning I couldn't remember what the heck the guy said.

When I left the Air Force I went into the Navy, and this is where everything began to happen for me. I had originally intended to just go from service to service and do something that very few people have ever done before. I was a very adventurous, very crazy...young man, and I thought that it would be a pretty exciting life.

I volunteered for submarines, and while on the submarine USS Tiru, SS-416, on a transit between the Portland/Seattle area and Pearl Harbor, which was our home port; the Pearl Harbor sub base, as the port lookout I saw a craft, saucer-shaped, the size of a Midway class carrier, aircraft carrier, for those of you who don't know how big that is; it's huge, come up out of the water approximately two 1/2 nautical miles off the port bow, which is about 45 degrees to the left of the pointy end of the submarine.

It tumbled slowly on its own axis, and went up into the clouds. It appeared to be moving slowly to me at a distance of two 1/2 nautical miles, but in reality it was moving pretty fast because it came up out of the water, did a few tumbles and it was gone!

I then reported it to the officer of the deck. I didn't tell him what it was that I saw because my Daddy didn't raise no fools and in case nobody else saw it I didn't want to be the only loony onboard the ship. So I asked the officer of the deck to help me cover that area, and he did, which is common for officers and lookouts to help each other while on bridge watch because they all hang together if something bad happens. After a few seconds of watching, the same craft, or another craft exactly like it, came down out of the clouds, tumbled again on its own axis, and went into the water.

Ensign Ball, who was the officer of the deck, was literally shocked! What could I say? Seaman Geromio, who was the starboard lookout, had also witnessed this, and ensign Ball called the captain to the bridge who was followed by the chief quartermaster who brought a 35MM camera, and we watched for between seven and 10 minutes the same craft, or different craft that looked exactly alike, enter and leave the water. It was an incredible show.

I don't know if they knew we were there, or if they even cared, but the craft did not glow, they were metal, they were machines without a doubt, they were obviously intelligently guided, they were HUGE, and having been in the Air Force and the Navy and knowing what it takes, I knew without a doubt, and know it today, that machine was not made on the face of this Earth. Because there's nothing that man can make, that can fly through the air at a speed like that, tumble on its own axis, and enter the water and effectively fly under the sea.

If you've ever been aboard an airplane and then gone aboard a submarine, I know there's probably some of you in this room who have visited a submarine at one time or another, you can readily see just without even any of the technicalities involved how difficult such a thing would be to do. Where would it be built, that size? It was absolutely incredible. It changed my life because then all the stories that I'd heard all my life I knew were true, and I began seeing the world in a different light. It wasn't long after that I was trained by Naval security in intelligence.

I was sent to Viet Nam. I was assigned as a patrol boat captain, first in Da Nang harbor, given a crew, given a multi-million dollar patrol boat. My job was to gather intelligence from the people who lived around the harbor and the fishermen who transited the harbor, and maintain the safety and security of the harbor and the shipping. After about 5 months, I was sent up North to the DMZ, to a place called Qua Viet, on the Thack Han River.

Our base camp was at the river mouth. We were only three miles South of the North Vietnamese border and our job was to patrol the Thack Han river from the river mouth to
Dong Ha, and then up the Quang Tree cutoff to Quang Tree city, again to get to know the people on the bank, gather intelligence, and to patrol every night and maintain the safety and security of the river and the river traffic.

WILLIAM COOPER: DEATH OF A CONSPIRACY SALESMAN

It was while there that I discovered that there was a tremendous amount of UFO and alien activity in Viet Nam. It was always reported in official messages as "enemy helicopters." Now any of you who know anything about the Viet Nam war know that the North Vietnamese did not have any helicopters, especially after our first couple of air raids into North Viet Nam. Even if they had they would not have been so foolish as to bring them over the DMZ because that would have insured their demise.

Our troops were fired on occasionally by these enemy helicopters, enemy troops were fired on occasionally by these enemy helicopters, and occasionally people would disappear. And on one instance that I know for sure at least one entire village disappeared one night due to alien activity. The reason they used the term enemy helicopters in messages and dispatches was that in Viet Nam you could be overrun at any time, no matter where you where. They did not bring crypto encoding equipment into Viet Nam, I'm talking about the machinery. What we did is we had crypto tables, and once we every 24-hours those codes would be no good. So that's what we used. We also, because of the inability to use crypto transmitting equipment, had to devise code words such as 'enemy helicopters.'

When I left Viet Nam I was eventually attached to the head-quarters staff of the Commander in Chief of the United States Pacific Fleet in Hawaii, which is on a little hill overlooking Pearl Harbor, it's a beautiful white building up there, and I was specifically attached to the Intelligence Briefing Team of the Commander in Chief of the United States Pacific Fleet.

It was during this tour of duty that, in the course of my duties, documents were placed in my hands that were so unbelievable and so incredible that it took me quite a while to adjust to the fact that what I was seeing was real. Now for those of you who don't understand how I could come to see this information let me give you a little short course in security clearance and "the need to know" and how you get to see classified information if you're in the military or in the government, it doesn't matter which, the rules are the same.

Number one you need a security clearance, and you've got to have clearance at the level that the information you want to see is classified at. In this instance it was classified "Top Secret, Magic, Restricted Information," which I came to find out later is the highest security classification in the Nation.

To get that type of clearance, all you have to have is a Federal Bureau of Investigation background check, which takes about six months and they send federal agents to your home, to your old schools, to all your teachers, to your friends, to everybody you put down on your security clearance forms, to all your old addresses, your neighbors, everybody that you've worked for, and it's embarrassing because they don't tell them what they're checking on. They just show them their identification and start asking questions and that's when you find out who's your friend and who's not, because a lot of people get scared and think, "Bill just robbed a bank and I'm not talking to him anymore."

Now once you get that it's called a 'B.I.' and for those of you who have received a copy of my service record look on the first page, the DD-214 where it says Security Clearance, you will see the term B.I. That's a Bureau of Investigation clearance. Now at that point, you have the clearance for everything including Top Secret and above. What determines what you get to see is your need to know, and the job that you have determines what your need to know is.

I was assigned to the Intelligence Briefing Team of the Commander in Chief of the United States Pacific Fleet, who had to know everything concerning his area of operations which was one-half of the Earth's surface; the Indian ocean, the Pacific ocean, and all the land masses in between. Believe it or not, if we go to war, if we ever go to war, it's the United States Navy that strikes the first blow and attempts to keep the enemy at bay while we can get ourselves together, at least historically. Nuclear weapons have kind of done away with that concept, but military commanders like to talk about it anyway.

Because of this, and you have no conception of the amount of material and information that an area commander has to know, it's unbelievable, and he has to keep track of this, he has to keep on top of it. He has to know what's happening, he has to make the right decisions. Because it's almost humanly impossible for anyone to do that, they have what's called a briefing team, and it's our job to make sure that he has the correct information, all the time, on a 24-hour basis. And every morning, between 8 and 9 AM, we would give a briefing which covered everything that happened in the previous 24-hours, and everything scheduled to happen in the next 24-hours, and all the pertinent intelligence reports that we had received since the last briefing that he needed to know and that his staff members needed to know.

Occasionally we would get messages marked "Top Secret, Magic, Restricted Information," and it would be coded in such a way that all you had were answers to questions which you didn't know what the questions were so you really didn't know what the message was all about.

But eventually I found myself in possession, holding two documents; one called Project Grudge, another one called Operation Majority. Project Grudge contained the history of alien involvement since around 1936, and it began talking about Germany's involvement with a crashed disk that they had recovered in 1936 and were attempting to duplicate the technology. They were not successful despite what all these Nazi hunters want to tell you. If they had been successful, we would not have won the war, because you cannot beat those weapons! You cannot out fly those craft, you can't even think about it with conventional aircraft. If Germany had been successful, we would now have a German flag up in front of this podium.

They did make some headway. When we went into Germany we captured documents, we got some scientists, we got some hardware. The Russians also got some documents, some scientists, and some hardware. It wasn't until 1947 that we were able to capture a craft, a whole craft, not all together but it was everything. And that occurred near the city of Roswell, New Mexico. There were dead aliens recovered from the craft. In Project Grudge I saw photographs of these dead aliens, of the craft, I saw photographs of live aliens, I saw photographs of autopsies, internal organs, I saw photographs of the alien designated EBE which was held in captivity from 1949 until June the 2nd, 1952 when he died. I saw the history of what they had been able to at that time put together, from incidents in the 1800's which involved aliens and their craft.

I saw the names of projects. I saw a project that was to fly recovered alien craft that had been recovered intact and undamaged, and some of them were recovered intact and undamaged, and how that happened I have no idea. It was called Project Redlight, and first was conducted from the Tonopah test range in the Nevada test sight and then was moved to a specially built area, ordered built by president Eisenhower, called Area-51, code named Dreamland, in the Groom dry lake area of the Nevada test sight, by secret executive order. It doesn't exist officially, if you ask anyone, or if you write letters to the government they will tell you it doesn't exist. However if you go out there at several places and see it, fly outside the boundaries and look down and see it, you know it's there, but according to the government it doesn't exist.

The project to fly, test fly these craft, was ongoing until sometime in 1962 when a craft blew up not far from the test sight, in the air, and the explosion was seen over a three-state area. The pilots were killed, they had no idea what had happened or why the craft blew up, but they put Project Redlight on hold until a later date when the aliens supplied us with three craft and personnel to help us learn how to fly these craft. That project is ongoing and we now have not only alien craft that we are flying, we have craft we have built, using the captured technology, and some of the UFO's that people report seeing in the United States, and maybe even elsewhere, are flown by United States personnel. That may come as a shock to you. We have technology way beyond the limits of what we have been told. A lot of our development technologically, since the end of World War II, has been due to the exchange of technology which occurs in the area called Area-51 on a regular basis

When James Oberth, professor Oberth retired, many of you don't know who he is...not too many space people in here. Professor Oberth was probably one of the greatest rocket scientists that ever lived. When he retired, the government gave him a special award, there was a press conference, all kinds of ceremony, and when he got up to speak he said, "Gentlemen, we cannot take credit for all the technological developments that we have had in the last decade. We have had help," and that's where he stopped.

One of the reporters raised his hand and said, "Professor Oberth, can you tell us what other country helped us?"

He said, "It was those little guys from out in space." And then he got down and would not comment any further. Now this occurred in 1959. I can go on and on but time doesn't allow it. I will tell you ladies and gentlemen that there are all kinds of things going on all the time, we are making rapid progress in exposing this. Since I have begun talking, people have been coming out of the woodwork at a rapid rate, who know and have pieces of this puzzle, and are helping us to put it together, because I don't have all the answers. I saw an awful lot of material, I have remembered an awful lot of it, I have probably, in my remembering, made some mistakes, and I guarantee you they're minor ones, if I have.

We have just recently, for those of you who didn't believe that the Jason Society of the Jason Scholars, the secret group existed, we now have a letter from the Pentagon, with 51 names of the Jason Scholars, an admission from the Pentagon that they hold the highest security clearances in the nation, an admission from the Pentagon that they hold the protocol rank of Rear Admiral, and are treated as such on any military installation or in any government office. There are six Nobel Prize winners on that list, there are the elite of the elite of the scientific world, they are the only ones who really know the truth about the technology today and about the real science of physics, because the one that we're being taught all the time.

If you send your kids to college to learn physics you're wasting your money because they're teaching them stuff that doesn't work, it's not true. Gravity is not what we think it is. There IS a Unified Theory! We already know what it is, it's what makes these craft work.

How many of you keep up with Billy Goodman's show on KVEG out of Las Vegas? For those of you who don't, I would try tuning in on any night between 10:00 PM and 1:00 AM. It's 840 on your AM dial, and the subject every night are those subjects that no other media person in the United States will touch with a ten-foot pole, every single night except Saturday night. It's

WILLIAM COOPER: DEATH OF A CONSPIRACY SALESMAN

the only show that you can call in and talk to another caller, you've got three minutes to say whatever you want to say as long as you don't cuss or swear or slander anyone, and every night they're helping to expose this.

When John Lear and I first said what was going on out at Groom Lake everybody said, "You're nuts, there's nothing going on out at Groom Lake!" The listeners of the Billy Goodman radio show put together an excursion and went up to Groom Lake and they all, ever since, every night, they go up there and watch them test fly the alien craft ...every night!

The first night they had 100 people there. And 100 people saw four alien craft fly, doing things that no airplane and no helicopter can do. Now they don't tell us anymore that there's nothing happening at Groom Lake. What they tell us now is there's no such thing as aliens, it's all government secret projects. That's okay because we'll prove that wrong too eventually, it just takes awhile. Because where we were...it's not where we're at, and I'm really happy about that.

Now, if you want to see what's happening right now, keep watching your movies, keep watching your television commercials, your alien programs on television, read Whitley Strieber's book *Majestic* which is a part of the contingency plan called "Majestic" to test the reaction of the population to the presence of aliens on the Earth. Having just finished Strieber's book, I'm gonna tell you right now that most of the documents in there, that he says are fiction, are real documents that came right out of Project Grudge. It is part of the government's campaign to leak information out in ways that they can always deny that it's real.

This is gonna come out, and the reason they're doing it the way they're doing it is they know eventually you're gonna find out that it's all true and real. They're desensitizing you so that you're not shocked, so that there's no collapse of society as we know it, so that the religious structure doesn't fall to pieces, so that the stock market doesn't go crazy, because these were their original fears. Now, there's nothing we can do about the last one because it's already happened, there will be a segment of the population that worships the aliens, even though they're no different than us they're just from somewhere else, and they may look a little different. They are not gods. But there are already people worshiping the aliens and they predicted this would happen when they slapped the secret stamp all over all this stuff.

You know, there's really nothing wrong with what's been happening except for two things; Number one, when they decided to keep it secret they needed to finance it, they couldn't tell the public so they couldn't tell Congress. They decided to finance it with the sale, importation and sale, of drugs. Now in the documents that I read, in Operation Majority, it specifically stated that when

61

WILLIAM COOPER: DEATH OF A CONSPIRACY SALESMAN

George Bush was the president and CEO of a certain oil company, he, in conjunction with the CIA, organized the first large scale drug importation into this country from South and Central America by fishing boat, to offshore oil platforms, and then from there into the beach, thus bypassing all Customs inspections and law enforcement inspections of any kind. They are still bringing in drugs, to a limited extent, in this manner.

Another manner is by CIA contract aircraft which, one of their bases of landing is Homestead Air Force Base in Florida. We have affidavits from air controllers who have vectored the planes in, who have made sure that they're not interfered with in any way. We have affidavits from personnel at Homestead Air Force Base who say the planes have been met by Zeb Bush, who's George Bush's son. We have affidavits from people who work in the Gulf of Mexico, in the offshore oil business, that yes indeed, the drugs are coming in, at least some of them, from the offshore oil platforms.

Now, that's one of the things that's wrong. The next thing that's wrong is, to keep the secret, they killed a lot of people who tried to leak it out. And if I hadn't done it the way that I did it, you wouldn't be seeing me anywhere standing or walking on this Earth now. They killed President Kennedy and during the workshop, for those of you haven't seen the tape, I will show you, on the tape, who shot the President and why.

Between '70 and '73, in Operation Majority it stated verbatim that President Kennedy ordered MJ-12 to cease the importation and sale of drugs to the American people, that he ordered them to implement a plan to reveal the presence of aliens to the American people within the following year. His assassination was ordered by the policy committee of the Bilderbergers. MJ-12 implemented the plan and carried it out in Dallas. It involved agents of the CIA, Division-5 of the FBI, the Secret Service, and the office of Naval Intelligence.

President Kennedy was killed by the driver of his car, his name was William Greer, he used a recoilless, electrically operated, gas-powered assassination pistol that was specially built by the CIA to assassinate people at close range. It fired an explosive pellet which injected a large amount of shellfish poison into the brain, and that is why, in the documents, it stated that President Kennedy's brain was removed. If you've studied the case, you will find that indeed his brain has disappeared.

The reason for that is so that they would not find the particles of the exploding pellet or the shellfish poison in his brain which would have proved conclusively that Lee Harvey Oswald was not the assassin. In fact, Lee Harvey Oswald never fired a shot, he was the patsy.

WILLIAM COOPER: DEATH OF A CONSPIRACY SALESMAN

There were a total of three shots fired at President Kennedy, one hit him in the throat and didn't kill him and two of them hit Gov. John Connally. The one that was fired from the grassy knoll hit the president in the throat. The other two shots came from directly behind the limousine, not the school book depository building, and hit Connally. Connally, in intelligence community circles, is known as a "can do" man, because he took two hits and still kept his mouth shut.

For those of you who have been listening to all these talk show hosts, whose job it is to be a talk show host, and who have not done any legitimate research into this, if you come to the workshop, I will show you, on the tape, how it was done by the driver. You will see that Kennedy was, in fact slumped over against Jackie, his head was turned [this direction], it was very simple, it was easy and you will see it with your own eyes. Most of the Zapruder film that you can purchase has that segment cut out, and you can always tell it by the person running in the background, they'll run up to here... all of a sudden they'll be down here running. You will see in most of the clips that you've ever seen on television, or in the movies, or that you're able to get your hands on, you'll see William Greer start to turn like this and shoot Kennedy.

What you need to do is what you should have been doing all along. You need to get involved with your government. The first thing you need to do is purchase a copy of the Constitution, which I know that most of you don't have anywhere in your house, and if I were to go around this room and ask each person what the Constitution says, most of you couldn't tell me what the Constitution says from your grocery bill. And that's the truth! And that IS your country! So if you don't know what your Constitution is you're dead already, so the first thing you do is you get a copy of your Constitution.

The second thing you do is you learn it! The third thing you do is you start calling your senators and your representatives, and the President of the United States and you start leaning on them, and you tell them, "Unless you straighten up the government, and unless we start getting the truth, and I mean the whole truth, and no more of this baloney, this is the last job you're ever gonna have, period. And I'll do everything in my power to make sure that comes true." And then write them, frequently, saying the same thing. And then when they're in your area, in their area offices, take a little delegation and go see them, and make them understand that they're gonna be living in poverty because they're not gonna have a job anymore come election day.

You see, the secret government may own the executive branch, but you people, all of us, we own the Congress, and the Congress makes the laws, and the Congress can impeach the entire executive branch! You also have the right to petition the government for a redress of injuries. So you ARE powerful, you've just forgotten that you're powerful, you've forgotten that vote that you haven't been doing every time election comes around, that vote has abdicated your power. That vote you did not cast abdicated your power and gave it to those who are subverting the Constitution and are ruining this country.

[A gentleman from the audience asked, "What did we trade to the aliens for their technology, and is the Soviet Union in on any of this?"]

People and animals, replied Cooper succinctly. The Soviet Union and the United States of America have been close allies since the end of World War II and have been closely participating in the secret space program all this time. The Soviets have the same thing we have, yes. What you see happening in the Soviet block right now is not the result of people standing up and saying, "We want to be free." It's the result of the international bankers saying, "You tear down these barriers, and you meet the West half way, give your people some freedom, the West is gonna take some freedom away from their people so that we can put together a one-world economic system...and have all the power." That's what's happening! If you don't believe it, stick around and watch it!

Another reason that Kennedy may have been killed was the possibility that he was going to blow the whistle on the militaries secret space program. The first Mars landing was May the 22nd, 1962 with a winged probe that used a hydrazine propeller, flew around approximately three orbits and landed on the surface. This was a joint United States / Russian endeavor. The first time that we landed on the moon was sometime during the middle 50's, because at the time when President Kennedy stated that he wanted a man to set foot on the moon by the end of the decade we already had a base there.

We have a base on Mars also. I don't know the exact date that the Mars Base was constructed, but I know the project's name, it was "Adam and Eve." I revealed it publicly for the first time on July the 2nd, 1989, and within three weeks of the time I revealed it publicly, the government, to get the American people not to listen to me, came out and said that they planned to build a base on the moon and a colony on Mars. This project is also known as Alternative 1, 2 and 3, and it is very real.

William Cooper at a lecture in Hawaii: "I saw a project that was to fly recovered alien craft that had been recovered intact and undamaged. These UFOs were tested at Area 51 in Nevada." **Photos Courtesy Sherry Hansen Steiger**

7.

Secret Societies/New World Order by Milton William Cooper

History is replete with whispers of secret societies. Accounts of elders or priests who guarded the forbidden knowledge of ancient peoples. Prominent men, meeting in secret, who directed the course of civilization are recorded in the writings of all people.

The oldest is the Brotherhood of the Snake, also called the Brotherhood of the Dragon, and it still exists under many different names. It is clear that religion has always played a significant role in the course of these organizations. Communication with a higher source, often divine, is a familiar claim in all but a few.

The secrets of these groups are thought to be so profound that only a chosen, well-educated few are able to understand and use them. These men use their special knowledge for the benefit of all mankind. At least that is what they claim. How are we to know, since their knowledge and actions have been secret? Fortunately, some of it has become public knowledge.

I found it intriguing that in most, if not all, primitive tribal societies all of the adults are members. They are usually, but not always, separated into male and female groups. The male usually dominates the culture. Surprisingly, this exactly resembles many civilized secret societies. This can only mean that the society is working not against established authority, but for it.

In fact, could be said to actually be the established authority. This would tend to remove the validity of any argument that all secret associations are dedicated to the "destruction of properly constituted authority." This can only apply, of course, where the secret society makes up the majority or entirety of any people which it affects. Only a very few fall into this category.

Secret societies in fact mirror many facets of ordinary life. There is always an exclusivity of membership, with the resultant importance attached to being or becoming a member. This is found in all human endeavors, even those which are not secret, such as football teams or country clubs. This exclusivity of membership is actually one of the secret societies' most powerful weapons. There is the use of signs, passwords and other tools. These have always performed valuable functions in man's organizations everywhere. The stated reason, almost always different from the real reason, for the societies' existence is important.

The comradeship is especially important. Sharing hardships or secrets has always been a special thrill to man. No one who undergone the rigors of boot camp is ever likely to forget the special feeling of belonging and comradeship that was shared between the victims of the drill sergeant or company commander. It is an emotion born of initiation. The most potent tool of any secret society is the ritual and myth surrounding initiation. These special binding ceremonies have very deep meaning for the participants.

Initiation performs several functions which make up the heart and soul of any true secret society. Like boot camp, the initiation into the armed forces, important aspects of human thought that are universally compelling, are merged to train and maintain the efforts of a group of people to operate in a certain direction. Initiation bonds the members together in mysticism.

Neophytes gain knowledge of a secret, giving them special status. The ancient meaning of neophyte is "planted anew or reborn." A higher initiation is in reality a promotion inspiring loyalty and the desire to move up to the next rung. The goals of the society are reinforced, causing the initiated to act toward those goals in everyday life. That brings about a change in the political and social action of the member. The change is always in the best interest of the goals of the leaders of the secret society. The leaders are called adepts. This can best be illustrated by the soldier trained to follow orders without thinking. The result is often the wounding or death of the soldier for the realization of the commander's goal which may or may not be good for the overall community.

Initiation is a means of rewarding ambitious men who can be trusted. You will notice that the higher the degree of initiation the fewer the members who possess the degree. This is not because the other members are not ambitious but because a process of very careful selection is being conducted. A point is reached where no effort is good enough without a pull up by the higher members. Most members never proceed beyond this point and never learn the real, secret purpose of the group. The frozen member from that point on serves only as a part of the political power base as indeed he has always done. You may have guessed by now that initiation is a way to determine who can and cannot be trusted.

A method of deciding exactly who is to become an adept decided during initiation by asking the candidate to spit upon the Christian cross. If the candidate refuses, the members congratulate him and tell him, "You have made the right choice, as a true adept would never do such a terrible thing." The newly initiated might find it disconcerting, that he/she never advances any higher. If instead, the candidate spits upon the cross, he/she has demonstrated a knowledge of one of the mysteries and soon will find him/herself a candidate for the next higher level. The mystery is that religion is but a tool to control the masses. Knowledge (or wisdom) is their only god, through which man himself will become god. The snake and the dragon are both symbols of wisdom. Lucifer is a personification of the symbol. It was Lucifer who tempted Eve to entice Adam to eat of the tree of knowledge and thus free man from the bonds of ignorance. The worship (a lot different from study) of knowledge, science, or technology is Satanism in its purest form, its secret symbol is the all-seeing eye in the pyramid.

Undesirable effects of secret societies and their aura of mystery has sometimes given them the reputation for being abnormal associations or, at the very least, strange groups of people. Whenever their beliefs are those of the majority they are no longer considered antisocial. A good example is the Christian church, which was at one time a secret society under the Roman Empire. In fact, the "Open Friendly Secret Society" (the Vatican) actually ruled most, if not all, of the known world at one time.

Most secret societies are generally considered to be antisocial; they are believed to contain elements that are not liked or are outright harmful to the community in general. This is exactly the case in some instances. Communism and fascism are secret societies in many countries where they are prohibited by law. In this country the Nazi party and the Ku Klux Klan are secret societies due mostly to the fact that the general public is disgusted by them. Their activities are sometimes illegal, thus the secrecy of their membership.

The early Christians were a secret society because Roman authorities considered them from the start to be dangerous to imperial rule. The same was true of the followers of Islam. The Druseed and Yezidis in Syria and Iraq consider the Arabs a dangerous secret society dedicated to the takeover of the world. The Arabs today think the same of the Jews. Catholics and Freemasons used to have precisely the same ideas about each other.

In many primitive or backward societies initiation into the highest degrees of the group involved subjection to trials which not infrequently resulted in death or insanity for the candidate. It can be seen that social right and wrong is not the yardstick in estimating the value of a secret society. In Borneo, initiates of hunting societies, consider it meritorious and compulsory to hunt heads. In Polynesia, infanticide and debauch were considered essential for initiation into their societies, where the tribal code needed members who indulged in these things, as pillars of society.

Since the beginning of recorded history, governmental bodies of every on have been involved with maintaining the status quo to defend the establishment against minority groups that sought to function as states within states or to oust the constituted authority and take over in its place. Many of these attempts have succeeded but have not always lasted. Man's desire to be one of the elect is something that no power on earth has been able to lessen, let alone destroy. It is one of the "secrets" of secret societies. It is what gives them a political base and lots of clout. Members often vote the same and give each other preference in daily business, legal, and social activities. It is the deepest desire of many to be able to say, "I belong to the elect."

Houses of worship and sacrifice existed in the ancient cities. They were in fact temples built in honor of the many gods. These buildings functioned often as meeting places for philosophers and mystics who were believed to possess the secrets of nature. These men usually banded together in seclusive philosophic and religious schools.

The most important of all of these ancient groups is the Brotherhood of the Snake, or Dragon, and was simply known as the Mysteries. The snake and dragon are symbols that represent wisdom. The father of wisdom is Lucifer, also called the Light Bearer. The focus of worship for the Mysteries was Osiris, the name of a bright star that the ancients believed had been cast down onto the earth. The literal meaning of Lucifer is "bringer of light" or "the morning star." After Osiris was gone from the sky, the ancients saw the Sun as the representation of Osiris ("...it is claimed that, after Lucifer fell from Heaven, he brought with him the power of thinking as a gift for mankind." Fred Gittings, *Symbolism in Occult Art*)

Most of the greatest minds that ever lived were initiated into the society of Mysteries by secret and dangerous rites, some of which were very cruel. Some of the most famous were known as Osiris, Isis, Sabazius, Cybele and Eleusis. Plato was one of these initiates and he describes some of the mysteries in his writings.

Plato's initiation encompassed three days of entombment in the Great Pyramid, during which time he died (symbolically), was reborn, and was given secrets that he was to preserve. Plato's writings are full of information on the Mysteries. Manly P. Hall stated in his book, ***The Secret Teachings of All Ages,*** that, "...the illumined of antiquity... entered its (pyramid of Giza) portals as men; they came forth as gods." The ancient Egyptian word for pyramid was khuti, which meant "glorious light." Mr. Hall says also, "The pyramids, the great Egyptian temples of initiation..."

According to many, the great pyramids were built to commemorate and observe a supernova explosion that occurred in the year 4000 B.C. Dr. Anthony Hewish, 1974 Nobel Prize winner in physics, discovered a rhythmic series of radio pulses which he proved were emissions from a star that had exploded around 4000 B.C. The Freemasons begin their calendar from A.L., "In the Year of Light," found by adding 4000 to the modern year. Thus 1990 + 4000 = 5990 A.L. George Michanowsky wrote in The Once and Future Star that "The ancient Sumerian cuneiform...described a giant star exploding within a triangle formed by...Zeta Puppis, Gamma Velorum, and Lambda

Velorum...located in the southern sky....[An] accurate star catalogue now stated that the blazing star that had exploded within the triangle would again be seen by man in 6000 years." According to the Freemason's calendar it will occur in the year 2000, and indeed it will.

The spacecraft called Galileo is on its way to Jupiter, a baby star with a gaseous makeup exactly the same as our sun, with a load of 49.7 pounds of plutonium, supposedly being used as batteries to power the craft. When its final orbit decays in December 1999, Galileo will deliver its payload into the center of Jupiter. The unbelievable pressure that will be encountered will cause a reaction exactly as occurs when an atomic bomb is exploded by an implosion detonator. The plutonium will explode in an atomic reaction, lighting the hydrogen and helium atmosphere of Jupiter and resulting in the birth of the star that has already been named Lucifer.

The world will interpret it as a sign of tremendous religious significance. It will fulfill prophecy. In reality it is only a demonstration of the insane application of technology by the JASON Society which may or may not even work. They have practiced overkill to ensure success, however, as the documents that I read while in Naval Intelligence stated that Project GALILEO required only five pounds of plutonium to ignite Jupiter and possibly stave off the coming ice age. Global warming is a hoax. It is easier for the public to deal with and will give the ruling elite more time before panic and anarchy replace government. The reality is that overall global temperatures are becoming lower. Storms are becoming more violent and less predictable.

The icecaps at the poles are growing larger. The temperate zones where food can be grown are shrinking. Desertification is increasing in the tropics. An ice age is on its way, and it will occur suddenly.

Simultaneously a vault containing the ancient records of the earth will opened in Egypt. The opening of the vault will usher in the millennium. A great celebration has already been planned by the Millennium Society to take place at the pyramids in Egypt. According to the January 3, 1989, edition of the *Arizona Daily Star*, President-elect Bush is spending this New Year's holiday at Camp David, Maryland, but in 10 years, according to the organizers of the Millennium Society, he may be in Egypt at the Great Pyramid of Cheops.

The first secret that one must know to even begin to understand the Mysteries is that their members believe that there are but few truly mature minds in the world. They believe that those minds belong exclusively to them. The philosophy that follows is the classic secret-society view of humanity:

WILLIAM COOPER: DEATH OF A CONSPIRACY SALESMAN

"When a person of strong intellect is confronted with a problem which calls for the use of reasoning faculties, they keep their poise and attempt to read a solution by garnering facts bearing upon the question. On the other hand, those who are immature, when confronted by the small problem, are overwhelmed. While the former may be said to be qualified to solve the mystery of their own destiny, the latter must be led like a bunch of animals and taught in the simplest language. Like sheep they are totally dependent upon the shepherd. The able intellect is taught the Mysteries and the esoteric spiritual truths. The masses are taught the literal, exoteric interpretations. While the masses worship the five senses, the select few observe, recognizing in the gulf between them the symbolic concretions of great abstract truths.

"The initiated elect communicate directly to Gods (ALIENS?) who communicate back to them. The masses sacrifice their lambs on an altar facing a stone idol that can neither hear or speak. The elect are given knowledge of the Mysteries and are illumined and are thus known as The Illluminati or the Illuminated Ones, the guardians of the Secrets of the Ages."

Three early secret societies that can be directly connected to a modern descendant are the cults of Roshaniya, Mithras and their counterpart, the Builders. They have many things in common with the Freemasons of today as well as with many other branches of the Illuminati. For instance, common to the Brotherhood are the symbolic rebirth into a new life without going through the portal of death during initiation; reference to the "Lion" and "the Grip of the Lion's Paw" in the Master Mason's degree; the three degrees, which is the same as the ancient Masonic rites before the many other degrees were added; the ladder of seven rungs; men only; and the "all-seeing eye."

Of special interest is the powerful society in Afghanistan in ancient times called the Roshaniya - illuminated ones. There are actually references to this mystical cult going back through history to the House of Wisdom at Cairo. The major tenets of this cult were: the abolition of private property; the elimination of religion; the elimination of nation states; the belief that illumination emanated from the Supreme Being who desired a class of perfect men and women to carry out the organization and direction of the world; belief in a plan to reshape the social system of the world by first taking control of individual countries one by one, and the belief that after reaching the fourth degree one could communicate directly with the unknown supervisors who had imparted knowledge to initiates throughout the ages. Wise men will again recognize the Brotherhood.

The important fact to remember is that the leaders of both the right and the left are a small, hard core of men who have been and still are Illuminists or members of the Brotherhood. They may have been or may be members of the

Christian or Jewish religions, but that is only to further their own ends. They give allegiance to no particular nation, although they have used nationalism to further their causes. Their only concern is to gain greater economic and political power. The ultimate objective of the leaders of both groups is identical. They are determined to win for themselves undisputed control of the wealth, natural resources, and manpower of the entire planet. They intend to turn the world into their conception of a totalitarian socialist state. In the process they will eliminate all Christians, Jews, and atheists. You have just learned one, but only one, of the great mysteries.

The Roshaniya also called themselves the Order. Initiates took an oath that absolved them of all allegiance except to the Order and stated, "I bind myself to perpetual silence and unshaken loyalty and submission to the Order. All humanity which cannot identify itself by our secret sign is our lawful prey."

The oath remains essentially the same to this day. The secret sign was to pass a hand over the forehead, palm inward; the countersign, to hold the ear with the fingers and support the elbow in the cupped other hand. Does that sound familiar?

The Order is the Order of the Quest. The cult preached that there was a spirit state completely different from life as we know it. The spirit could continue to be powerful on earth through a member of the Order, but only if the spirit had been itself a member of the Order before its death. Thus members of the Order gained power from the spirits of the dead members.

The Roshaniya took in travelers as initiates and then sent them on their way to found new chapters of the Order. It is believed by some that the Assassins were a branch of the Roshaniya. Branches of the Roshaniya or "the illuminated ones" or the Illuminati existed and still exist everywhere. One of the rules was not to use the same name and never mention "the Illuminati." That rule is still in effect today. I believe that it is the breaking of this rule that resulted in Adam Weishaupt's downfall.

One of the greatest secrets of the ages is the true story of the Holy Grail, the robe of Jesus, the remains of the Cross of Crucifixion, and whether Jesus actually died or if he survived and produced a child. Many myths surround the Knights Templar concerning these relics, and most myths throughout history always have at least some basis in fact. If my sources are correct, the Knights Templar survive today as a branch of the Illuminati and guard the relics, which are hidden in a location known only to them.

We know that the Templars are Illuminati because the Freemasons absorbed and protected those that escaped persecution of the church and France, just as the Freemasons would absorb and protect Weishaupt's Illuminati centuries later. The Knights Templar exist today as a high degree of

Freemasonry within the Templar Order. In fact, the Knights Templar is a branch of the Order of the Quest.

The DeMolay Society is branch of the Freemasons that consecrates the memory of the persecution of the Knights Templar and in particular, their leader Jacques deMolay. I know, because I was a member of the DeMolay Society as a young adult. I loved the mystery and ritual. I became separated from the Society when my family moved to a location out of reach of any lodge. I believe to this day that my association with the DeMolay Society may have been the reason for my selection for Naval Security and Intelligence.

According to members of the intelligence community, when the New World Order is solidified the relics will be taken out, will be united with the Spear of Destiny, and will, according to legend, give the world's ruler absolute power. This may confirm beliefs passed down through the ages that describe the significance of these relics when united in the hands one man. It explains Hitler's desperate search World War II. (Gen. Patton had claimed it after defeat)

The Knights Templar were founded sometime during the 11th cent, in Jerusalem by the Prieure de Sion for the express purpose of guarding remaining relics of Jesus and to provide military protection for the religious travelers during their pilgrimage to the Holy City.

The Prieure de Sion was a religious order founded upon Mount Sion in Jerusalem. The Order set for itself the goal of preserving and recording the bloodline of Jesus and the House of David. Through every means available to them, the Prieure de Sion had found and retrieved the remaining relics. These relics were entrusted to the Knights Templar for safekeeping.

I am amazed at the authors of Holy Blood, Holy Grail and the information that they have unearthed. Most of all I am amazed at their inability to put the puzzle together. The treasure hidden in France is not the treasure of the Temple of Jerusalem. It is the Holy Grail itself,
the robe of Jesus, the last remaining pieces of the Cross of Crucifixion, and, according to my sources, someone's bones. I can tell you that the reality of the bones will shake the world to its very foundations if I have been told the truth. The relics are hidden in France. I know the location and so do the authors of Holy Blood, Holy Grail, but they do not know that they know - or do they?

Adam Weishaupt, a young professor of canon law at Ingolstadt University in Germany, was a Jesuit priest and an initiate of the Illuminati. The branch of the Order he founded in Germany in 1776 was the same Illuminati previously discussed. The Jesuit connection is important, as you will see later in this chapter. Researchers agree that he was financed by the House of Rothschild (mentioned in Silent Weapons for Quiet Wars). Weishaupt advocated "abolition of all ordered national governments, abolition of inheritance, abolition of private property, abolition of patriotism, abolition of the individual home and family life as the cell from which all civilizations have stemmed, and abolition of all religions established and existing so that the ideology of totalitarianism may be imposed on mankind."

In the same year that he founded the Illuminati he published Wealth of Nations, the book that provided the ideological foundation for capitalism and for the Industrial Revolution. It is no accident that the Declaration of Independence was written in the same year. On the obverse of the Great Seal of the United States the wise will recognize the all-seeing eye and other signs of the Brotherhood of the Snake.

Every tenet was the same. Date and beliefs confirm that Weishaupt's Illuminati is the same as the Afghan Illuminated Ones and the other cults which called themselves "illuminated." The Alumbrados of Spain were the same as were the "illuminated" Guerinets of France. In the United States they were known as the Jacobin clubs. Secrets within secrets within secrets, but always at the heart is the Brotherhood.

I believe that Weishaupt was betrayed and set up for persecution because he ignored the rule that the word "illuminati" or the existence of the Brotherhood would never be exposed to public knowledge. His exposure and outlawing accomplished several goals of the still-hidden and still very powerful brotherhood.

It allowed members to debunk claims of its existence on the grounds that the Illuminati had been exposed and outlawed and thus was no longer a reality. It allowed members to deny allegations of conspiracy of any kind. The Brotherhood of the Snake is adept at throwing out decoys to keep the dogs at bay. Weishaupt may have been a fool - or he may have been doing exactly what he was told.

Weishaupt said, "The great strength of our Order lies in its concealment; let it never appear in its own name, but always covered by another name, and another occupation."

Allegations that the Freemason organizations were infiltrated by the Illuminati during Weishaupt's reign are hogwash. The Freemasons have always contained the core of Illuminati within their ranks, and that is why they so freely and so willingly took in and hid the members of Weishaupt's group. You cannot really believe that the Freemasons, if they were only a simple fraternal organization, would have risked everything, including their very lives, by taking in and hiding outlaws who had been condemned by the monarchies of Europe. It is mainly Freemason authors who have perpetuated the myth that Adam Weishaupt was the founder of the Illuminati and that the Illuminati was destroyed, never to surface again.

In 1826 an American Freemason wrote a book revealing Masonic secrets entitled *Illustrations of Freemasonry*. One of the secrets that he revealed is that the last mystery at the top of the Masonic pyramid is the worship of Lucifer. We have since learned the secret of the "story of the murder of Hiram Abif." Hiram Abif represents intelligence, liberty and truth, and was struck down by a blow to the neck with a rule, representing the suppression of speech by the church; then he was struck in the heart with the square, representing the suppression of belief by the State; and finally he was struck on the head by a maul, representing the suppression of intellect by the masses. Freemasonry thus equates the Church, the State, and the masses with tyranny, intolerance, and ignorance. What Morgan revealed was that the Freemasons were pledged to avenge Hiram Abif and that their plan was to strike down the Church, the State, and the freedom of the masses.

Morgan caused a small uproar against the Masons. The small uproar turned into a full blown anti-Freemason movement when the author, William Morgan, disappeared. Morgan had apparently been abducted and drowned in Lake Ontario. It was alleged that fellow Masons had done it, and that they deny to this day. Who else would have done it? I believe they murdered him.

The newspapers of the time state without reservation that he was murdered by Masons. The oath of initiation into the Freemasons states that if secrets are told, the initiate will be murdered. A nationwide furor ensued that resulted in the creation of an anti-Masonic political party in 1829 by Henry Dana Ward, Thurlow Weed, and William H. Seward. Interest in several anti-Masonic books was revived during that period, with the result that Freemasonry suffered a severe loss of membership. It lasted only a few years and by 1840 the anti-Masonic party was extinct. Time really does cure all ills.

We know that the British Freemasons are a totally self-serving group that discriminates in favor of its own whenever jobs, promotions, contracts, or careers are concerned. The English Freemason organization was used by the KGB to infiltrate and take over British Intelligence. British Intelligence is synonymous with Chatham House, more commonly known as the Royal Institute for International Affairs, the parent organization of the Council on Foreign Relations in the United States. The English state police, Scotland Yard, ordered its personnel not to join the Masons for fear the same would happen to them. Of course, you have been told all your life that the Freemasons are only a benevolent fraternal organization bent only on community service. Read on, O innocent one.

Probably the most notorious Freemason lodge is the P2 lodge in Italy. This group has been implicated in everything from bribery to assassinations. P2 is directly connected to the Vatican, the Knights of Malta, and to the U.S. Central Intelligence Agency. It is powerful and dangerous. The P2 lodge has succeeded in infiltrating the Vatican and has scored a coup of tremendous significance: the Pope, John Paul II, has lifted the ban against Freemasonry. Many high-level members of the Vatican are now Freemasons.

I tell you now that Freemasonry is one of the most wicked and terrible organizations upon this earth. The Masons are major players in the struggle for world domination. The 33rd Degree is split into two. One split contains the core of the Luciferian Illuminati and the other contains those who have no knowledge of it whatsoever.

All of the intelligence officers that I worked for while in Naval Intelligence were Masons. As I stated before, I believe that my association with the DeMolay Society as a young adult may have been the reason that I was selected for Naval Security and Intelligence. However, that is only a guess.

I had intended to go into great detail linking P2, the Prieure de Sion, the Vatican, the CIA, organizations for a United Europe, and the Bilderberg Group. Fortunately, Michael Baigent, Righard Leigh & Henry Lincoln beat me to it. I say fortunately, because they confirm my previous allegation that I published in my paper The Secret Government that the CIA had plants, called moles, deep within the Vatican. You must read **Holy Blood, Holy Grail** and **The Messianic Legacy**, both by Baigent, Leigh, & Lincoln. Any reputable bookstore should carry them. Between pages 343 and 361 of **The Messianic Legacy** you can read of the alliance of power that resulted in a secret world government.

Most members of the Freemasons are not aware that the Illuminati practices what is known as "secrets within secrets," or organizations within organizations. That is one purpose of initiation. I cannot excuse any of the members, however, or anyone who joins a society without knowing everything about the organization is indeed a fool. Only those at the top who have passed every test truly know what the Masons are hiding, thus rendering it impossible for anyone outside to know much at all about the group. What does that say about new members or those who are already members but do not know the ultimate secrets? It tells me that fools abound.

Unlike authors who out of fear have acted as apologists for the Freemasons, I decline to absolve them of responsibility and guilt. The Freemasons, like everyone else, are responsible for the cleanliness of their home. The occupant of a secret house within a secret house within a secret house cannot clean if he cannot see the number of rooms or what they contain.

Their house is a stinking cesspool. Look to the Masons for the guilty party if anything happens to me. I believe that they have murdered in the past and that they will murder in the future.

Their goal is to rule the world. The doctrine of this group is not democracy or communism, but is a form of fascism. The doctrine is totalitarian socialism. You must begin to think correctly. The Illuminati are not Communists, but some Communists are Illuminati. (1) Monarchism (thesis) faced democracy (antithesis) in WWI, which resulted in the formation of communism and the League of Nations (synthesis). (2) Democracy and communism (thesis) faced fascism (antithesis) in WWII and resulted in a more powerful United Nations (synthesis). (3) Capitalism (thesis) now faces communism (antithesis) and the result will be the New World Order, totalitarian socialism (synthesis).

The 1953 report of the California Senate Investigating Committee on Education stated: "So-called modern Communism is apparently the same hypocritical world conspiracy to destroy civilization that was founded by the illuminati, and that raised its head in our colonies here at the critical period before the adoption of our Constitution." The California Senate understood that communism is the work of the Illuminati. They failed to realize that the Council on Foreign Relations and the Trilateral Commission are also the work of the Illuminati. You MUST begin to think correctly. The enemy is not communism, it is Illuminism. The Communists are not going to be much happier with the New World Order than we.

I hope to show that most modern secret societies and especially those that practice degrees of initiation, and that is the key, are really one society with one purpose. You may call them whatever you wish - the Order of the Quest, the JASON Society, the Roshaniya, the Qabbalah, the Knights Templar, the Knights of Malta, the Knights of Columbus, the Jesuits, the Masons, the Ancient and Mystical Order of Rosae Crucis, the Illuminati, the Nazi Party, the Communist Party, the Executive Members of the Council on Foreign Relations, The Group, the Brotherhood of the Dragon, the Rosicrucians, the Royal Institute of International Affairs, the Trilateral Commission, the Bilderberg Group, the Open Friendly Secret Society (the Vatican), the Russell Trust, the Skull & Bones, the Scroll & Key, the Order - they are all the same and all work toward the same ultimate goal, a New World Order.

Many of them, however, disagree on exactly who will rule this New World Order, and that is what causes them to sometimes pull in opposite directions while nevertheless proceeding toward the same goal. The Vatican, for instance, wants the Pope to head the world coalition. Some want Lord Maitreya to head the New World Order. Lord Maitreya is the front runner, I believe, since witnesses say he was present on the ship at Malta with Bush,

Gorbachev, and the ten regional heads of the New World Order. "Approximately 200 dignitaries from around the world attended a major conference initiated by Maitreya in London on April 21 and 22,1990. Representatives of governments (including the USA), members of royal families, religious leaders and journalists, all of whom had met with Maitreya previously, attended the conference." (Quote from Prophecy Watch column of *Whole Wheat* No. 8, Minneapolis)

Someone has also spent an awful lot of money announcing his presence. The Pope will have to approve him if Maitreya is selected, however, and that would fulfill the Bible prophecy in the Book of Revelation that states that the first beast will be given his power by Rome. If you can interpret Revelation as I can, then you know that the Pope will ultimately win out and will reign as the second beast.

In 1952 an alliance was formed, bringing them all together for the first time in history. The Black Families, the Illuminati (the Order), the Vatican, and the Freemasons now work together to bring about the New World Order. All will protest their innocence and will do everything within their power to destroy anyone who suggests otherwise. I will undoubtedly become a target when this book is published.

You may notice that some of those listed in the preceding paragraphs do not, or so it appears, practice degrees of initiation. That is the public view. Look at the Council on Foreign Relations. Many members - in fact, the majority - never serve on the executive committees. They never go through any initiation of any kind. They are, in fact, the power base and are used to gain a consensus of opinion.

The majority are not really members but are made to feel as if they are. In reality they are being used and are unwilling or unable to understand. The Executive Committee is an inner core of intimate associates, members of a secret society called the Order of the Quest, also known as the JASON Society, devoted to a common purpose. The members are an outer circle on whom the inner core acts by personal persuasion, patronage and social pressure. That is how they bought Henry Kissinger. Rockefeller gave Kissinger a grant of $50,000 in the early '50s, a fortune in those days, and made dear old Henry a member of the CFR.

Anyone in the outer circle who does not toe the mark is summarily expelled and the lesson is not lost on those who remain. Do you remember the human desire to be a member of the elect? That is the principle at work.

The real power are men who are always recruited without exception from the secret societies of Harvard and Yale known as the Skull & Bones and the Scroll & Key. Both societies are secret branches (also called the Brotherhood of Death) of what is otherwise historically known as the Illuminati. They are connected to parent organizations in England (The Group of Oxford University and especially All Souls College), and Germany (the Thule Society, also called the Brotherhood of Death).

I learned this when I was with Naval Intelligence. I was not able to explain why some members of the Executive Committee were not listed under the "Addresses" of Chapter 322 of the Skull & Bones Society until I read *The Wise Men* by Walter Isaacson & Evan Thomas, Simon and Schuster, New York. Under illustration #9 in the center of the book you will find the caption "Lovett with the Yale Unit, above far right, and on the beach: His initiation into Skull and Bones came at an air base near Dunkirk." I have found that members of these two societies were chosen on an ongoing basis by invitation based upon merit post-college and were not confined to only Harvard or Yale attendees.

Only members of the Order are initiated into the Order of the Quest, the JASON Society that makes up the executive members of the Council on Foreign Relations and, in fact, the Trilateral Commission as well. The executive members of the Council on Foreign Relations are the real elect in this country. George Bush is a member of the Order. Surprised? You shouldn't be. His father was also a member who helped finance Hitler.

It is important that you know that the members of the Order take an oath that absolves them from any allegiance to any nation or king or government or constitution, and that includes the negating of any subsequent oath of allegiance which they may be required to take. They swear allegiance only to the Order and its goal of a New World Order. George Bush (and his son, George W. Bush, who is now being groomed to be President) is not a loyal citizen of the United States but instead is loyal only to the destruction of the United States and to the formation of the New World Order. According to the oath Bush took when he was initiated into Skull & Bones, his oath of office as President of the United States of America means nothing.

I read while in Naval Intelligence that at least once a year, maybe more, two nuclear submarines meet beneath the polar icecap and mate together at an airlock. Representatives of the Soviet Union meet with the Policy Committee of the Bilderberg Group. The Russians are given the script for their next performance. Items on the agenda include the combined efforts in the secret space program governing Alternative 3. I now have in my possession official NASA photographs of a moonbase in the crater Copernicus.

This method of meeting is the only way that is safe from detection and/or bugging. The public outcry that would result would destroy everything should these meetings be discovered. A BBC-TV documentary program entitled

Science Report revealed these same facts but subsequently issued a retraction. In their retraction they stated that the show had been fiction. It must be noted here that Science Report was a very respected documentary, nonfiction program in Britain.

Never in its history had it ever aired fiction. This subject is explored in depth in another chapter. There is no other method that I know of to verify these meetings short of somehow becoming a crew member on one of the submarines. Is Alternative 3 true, or is it a part of the plan to ring in the New World Order? It really doesn't matter, because either way we're screwed. The quicker you understand that, the wiser you become.

The members of the Bilderberg Group are the most powerful financiers, industrialists, statesmen and intellectuals, who get together each year for a private conference on world affairs. The meetings are notorious for the cloak of secrecy they are held under. The headquarters office is in The Hague in Switzerland, the only European country never invaded or bombed during World Wars I and II. Switzerland is the seat of world power. The goal of the Bilderberg Group is a one-world totalitarian socialist government and economic system. Take heed, as time is running short.

You must understand that secrecy is wrong. The very fact that a meeting is secret tells me that something is going on that I would not approve. Do not ever believe that grown men meet on a regular basis just to put on fancy robes, hold candles, and glad-hand each other. George Bush, when he was initiated into the Skull & Bones, did not lie naked in a coffin with a ribbon tied around his genitalia and yell out the details of all his sexual experiences because it was fun. He had much to gain by accepting initiation into the Order, as you can now see. These men meet for important reasons, and their meetings are secret because what goes on during the meetings would not be approved by the community. The very fact that something is secret means there is something to hide.

John Robison wrote Proofs of a Conspiracy in 1798, and I believe he said it best in the following passage from the book. "Nothing is so dangerous as a mystic Association. The object remaining a secret in the hands of the managers, the rest simply put a ring in their own noses, by which they may be led about at pleasure; and still panting after the secret they are the better pleased the less they see of their way. A mystical object enables the leader to shift his ground as he pleases, and to accommodate himself to every current fashion or prejudice. This again gives him almost unlimited power; for he can make use of these prejudices to lead men by troops. He finds them already associated by their prejudices, and waiting for a leader to concentrate their strength and set them in motion. And when once great bodies of men are set in motion, with a creature of their fancy for a guide, even the engineer himself cannot say, 'Thus far shalt thou go, and no farther.'"

Is the common man really as stupid as the elite seem to believe? If he is, then maybe the average citizen is better off ignorant, being manipulated this way and that, whenever the elite deem it necessary. We will discover the answer very quickly when the common man finds that his ticket to Fantasy Land has just expired.

8.
William Coopers Big List of Conspiracies

THE UFO CONSPIRACY

Caution is advised when delving into uFOOLogy. Most associated with this field are government agents, members of the Mysteries, con-artists, fakes, frauds, or just nuts. There are very few legitimate researchers and even less legitimate research. Finding the truth amid this mountain of lies, insanity, foolishness, fantasy, and misinformation is a monumental task.

Within MAJESTYTWELVE is Operation Majority justifying the plan by presenting an extraterrestrial threat as the reason for the necessity for world government ala "Who speaks for planet Earth...Argentina?"

Operation Majority is named after the original Bolshevik party which sparked the Russian Revolution. Bolshevik means the majority. The plan claims that if the American people are ever told of this extraterrestrial presence aliens will destroy the United States. All who have access to the plan or who inadvertently discover the plan are silenced by that warning. They believe in the government and thus believe the extraterrestrial lie. These dupes do not know that the Illuminati are the aliens who plan to destroy the United States of America in any event.

The natural skepticism of reporters insures that anyone who believes in extraterrestrial visitation or who links the so-called alien threat with the coming world government will be ridiculed and discredited.

When I saw Operation Majority while serving in the Navy I believed the alien threat was real just like everyone else. It was not until I had performed many years of research that I was able to fully understand exactly what it was that I had seen. It was extremely difficult for me to believe that my government and the United States Navy had used me, especially since I had dedicated my life to government and military service. Most government and military personnel cannot and will not believe such and idea.

The plan is real. The extraterrestrial threat is artificial. The threat is presented through the use of secret technology originally developed by the Germans in their secret weapons programs during WW-II, by geniuses like Nikola Tesla, and many others.

Military and government personnel who have access to this material believe it is real. None of them, however, has ever seen any evidence of the existence of any extraterrestrial creature nor any advanced technology other than that of human origin. It is not what they see that convinces them it is extraterrestrial in origin but the manner in which it is presented. It is extremely difficult, if not impossible, to believe that Top Secret government or military documentation could be lies. It is trust in government by men and women who have given their lives in its service that keeps this monumental lie a alive.

All so-called leaks are intentional misinformation projects designed to promote the alien threat scenario while allowing for complete deniability on the part of government. The plan to create an artificial extraterrestrial threat to the Earth was first mentioned by the Marxist, John Dewey. "Some one remarked that the best way to unite all the nations on this globe would be an attack from some other planet. In the face of such an alien enemy, people would respond with a sense of their unity of interest and purpose."

The premise was tested for credibility with the CBS presentation of War Of The Worlds on the CBS Radio Network by Orson Welles and the Mercury Theater. At 8:00 PM Eastern Standard Time, on the evening of October 30, 1938, the night before All Saints Day, now generally celebrated as Halloween, an estimated six million Americans listened to the famous Orson Welles broadcast, War Of The Worlds. The broadcast described an extraterrestrial invasion from Mars. An estimated one million sheople responded with sustained credulity and fear. Thousands responded with sheer panic.

The broadcast was a psychological warfare experiment conducted by The Princeton Radio Project. The Rockefeller Foundation funded the project in the fall of 1937. An Office of Radio Research was set up with Paul F. Lazarsfeld as director. Frank Stanton and Hadley Cantril were named associate directors. Cantril used a special grant from the General Education Board to study the effects of the broadcast. Cantril published the study as a book titled The Invasion From Mars - A Study In The Psychology Of Panic. It contains a complete script of the broadcast. The book is one of a series of studies sponsored by the Federal Radio Education Committee.

The public believed the War Of The Worlds was an actual news broadcast thus setting the stage for the implementation of an alien threat scenario. The only problem was that the state of the art of technology at that time did not allow for a believable presentation. The development of saucer shaped wingless and tailless flying machines by the Germans during WW-II and the implementation of psychological warfare against the sheople of the world solved the problem.

The artificial extraterrestrial threat was nurtured and built into an always present possibility over the next 50 years. Eventually a large percentage of the worlds population found themselves believing in alien ships, extraterrestrial visitation, alien mutilation of animals, and alien abductions of humans, with absolutely no substantial proof that extraterrestrials exist anywhere in the universe, much less that any have ever visited this isolated planet.

The artificial threat is further advanced through the mind control programming of Marxists and communists in Hollywood, radio, television, advertising, publishing houses, and the uFOOLogy movement all of which are in the complete control of the Illuminati and the Intelligence community. Fear is instilled through the incidental use of terror inspired by the cattle and animal mutilation by-products of the governments secret low level radiation monitoring, and the so-called alien abduction scenario induced by state-of-the-art and extremely sophisticated mind control operations.

THE DRUG CONSPIRACY

MAJESTYTWELVE revealed that drugs are brought into the United States by the Central Intelligence Agency, the military intelligence organizations, the Mossad, the KGB, and their partners in organized crime. The reasons given were to finance "black projects" that can never be revealed to Congress or oversight committees, and for social engineering. Within the past two years it has been revealed that Jewish Rabbis were at the head of drug organizations in New York and elsewhere, while other Rabbis provided the means of laundering drug money for others who imported and sold the drugs in order to finance their religious organizations or fund Israeli and Zionist projects.

Drugs have been a big help to the Illuminati's secret government. Society can be controlled by the control of drugs. This industry brings in unimaginable amounts of money which is accountable to no one. By making drugs plentiful at little or no price many people can be addicted and reduced to a form of euphemistic slavery under the complete control of the suppliers. An addict will do literally anything for a "fix." It is incomprehensible that the sheople actually wanted to elect Ollie North to the United States Senate after having been involved in trading cash for arms for drugs for more cash for more arms for more drugs...and delivering all those weapons to the enemies of the United States of America. It is my opinion that Ollie North is a disgrace to the uniform of the United States Marine Corp.

By making drugs hard to get and jacking up the price the controllers can create massive crime waves at anytime and at any place whenever they wish. These waves of crime frighten innocent law abiding People into agreeing to give up Rights and Freedoms in order to, "get the crime and drugs off the streets." Recent polls have claimed that a majority of the American People are willing to, "give up some of their Rights and Freedom in order to get the crime and drugs off the streets." After passing draconian legislation removing Rights and Freedoms the drugs are once again made plentiful and prices are lowered.

DEPARTMENT OF THE AIR FORCE
WASHINGTON DC 20330

OFFICE OF THE SECRETARY

19 December, 1990

Dear Mr.

LtCol. Cox requested that I write you, as you know the situation in the
Gulf has been occupying us round the clock. LtCol. Cox sends his regrets, but
as the situation stabilizes, he will be in touch.

First, there are still some concerns over the October issue of Av-Week.
We could not understand why they would run the Edwards story without review.
This is still under review. What are your ideas?

The Belgium situation has been corrected to all our satisfaction. I
understand that another show will air on the tabloid program that will show that
the sightings could be a mis-identification of terrestrial objects, say a street
light. This should air in January.

The Nevada situation has been brought under control by the inclusion of the
"porno" queen along with the Nellis allegations. That was a brilliant coup.
This entire issue is under constant monitoring. Anything else you may hear will
be of great interest.

The last area to be addressed concerns our "friend" Mr. Cooper. As you can
see by the attachment included, the reason for Mr. Cooper leaving Naval service.
I believe back in the old days, the phrase would be keel hauling. Cooper has
worked out beyond our expectations. With his paranoid personality, and alcohol
abuse not to mention the crowds he draws, we feel that the field has been
covered. Cooper, as expected, will self-destruct at some point, and with that,
a large part and parcel of this field will go with him. We were concerned last
year when he drew police interest in the vandalism case, but no charges were ever
filed. We still have assets that feed him bits and pieces that he weaves into
an ever more elaborate scenario. We are watching him closely, and if you hear
anything of interest we will look to hear from you. Thank you very much, and the
happiest of the Holiday Season to you and your family.

Sincerely,

Thomas Shively
Maj. USAF
S. & T. Group

1 Atch
1. Copy DD 214

**Alleged USAF document dated December 19, 1990, indicating that
William Cooper may have been part of the very government
disinformation campaigns that he preached against.**

And, what do you know...the crime disappears making the new laws look like they are actually working. This technique has been extensively used in the socialists war against the Second Amendment to the Constitution for the United States of America.

The first and largest drug smuggling operations were established on behalf of the CIA by George Herbert Walker Bush while he was the President and CEO of the offshore division of Zapata Oil. Fishing boats would deliver the drugs to the offshore rigs where they were transferred to helicopters and crew boats which were never inspected by customs or any other law enforcement agency. Most of the drugs flowing into the United States are owned and controlled by the CIA, the military intelligence organizations, and the Israeli Mossad.

TERRORISM/ANTHRAX/WAR IN THE MIDDLE EAST

In what would be his last public statements before his death - Cooper stated that MAJESTYTWELVE foretold that the first terrorist attack in the United States would occur in a large city such as New York. Based upon that statement Cooper accurately predicted that it would occur in New York, and it did when the World Trade Center was bombed.

MAJESTYTWELVE stated that terrorism would continue until the American People consented to be completely and thoroughly disarmed. The document stated that the second major target would be, "somewhere in the heartland such as Oklahoma City." The actual target was not named. Since the document was not specific as to the actual target and its location I did not predict Oklahoma City...but my prediction of continued terrorist attacks including major attacks upon the "heartland" of America was accurate.

The FBI appears to have orchestrated the attack upon the World Trade Center. Information was printed in the New York Times that proved the FBI taught the terrorists how to drive the van, build the bomb, place it in the building, and detonate the bomb. One of the FBI operatives/informants attempted to secure permission from the FBI to substitute inert ingredients so that no explosion would take place and no one could be injured.

The attack on the Alfred P. Murrah Federal Building was designed to affect the "Heartland" so that no one will feel safe. These acts in the manner of Hegel's Dialectic are leading to a need for the elimination of the Rights of individuals and the disarmament of all peoples so that the world supra government can step up to provide the solution which will be artificial safety and security from terrorism.

If these acts of terror do not succeed there will be more bombings, chemical, or biological attacks. They will escalate in the destruction, maiming and killing of men women and especially children. More shootings at shopping centers, restaurants, and schools will occur. As a last resort, if all else fails, the Illuminati are prepared to detonate an atomic weapon in a large American city such as New York, Chicago, or Los Angeles.

A war may be promulgated in the Middle East in order to provide the excuse needed to explain terrorist attacks upon the United States of America to the American sheople in order that they will accept personal disarmament in the interest of peace and security. Since the United States Army's announcement of the inoculation of all of its personnel with Anthrax vaccine I can safely predict that the next large terrorist event within the borders of the United States of America may be biological using Anthrax as the agent of destruction and death.

Saddam Hussein was trained by the CIA. Saddam Hussein was put in power in Iraq by the CIA under George Bush. The United States armed Iraq and gave Saddam Hussein the technology and scientific knowledge to create weapons of mass destruction. The United States sold Anthrax to Iraq.

The goal, of course, will be the destruction of national sovereignty worldwide, the establishment of a one world socialist government under the United Nations, disarmament of all nations, and the establishment of a world police force.

Who benefits from the World Trade Center and Pentagon terrorist attacks? I can tell you that no Arab nation benefits. I can tell you that no Muslim benefits. So why would any of them mount an attack that even the most stupid idiot fanatic in the world would understand to be the instrument of the absolute condemnation and alienation of his cause by all humanity?

Like most Americans I looked to the Arab world for the source of the attack, NOT because it was the most obvious solution, but because I have been programmed by the media to look only in that direction. I did not look elsewhere until stories appeared that set alarm bells ringing. Are we being deceived and manipulated? Who benefits from these attacks?

So who benefits? The answer is obvious and very disturbing. Everyone in the oil business will benefit, especially the Bush family and their business partners. Everyone in the defense industrial complex will benefit. The United Nations will benefit. The State of Israel will benefit big time. Tyranny in the name of security will benefit and rule over the American People. And don't be surprised if many Patriots and politically incorrect Americans begin to disappear overnight like the Jews and Gypsies in Nazi Germany.

The terrorists' attacks which will be launched in the United States will be blamed upon Middle Eastern religious fanatics, Christian fundamentalists, white supremacists, Patriots, or Militias. A more immediate result of these operations will be the increased use of military forces, weaponry, and equipment such as tanks and armored personnel carriers in civilian law enforcement, the suspension or elimination of Habeas Corpus, the elimination of jury trials, the attempted disarming of the American People, and the institution of martial law with show-trials conducted by a tribunal of judges.

PREDICTION - On 1/18/01 Bill Cooper stated on his website that he had been informed by several military officers that the U.S. will be involved in a major war in the Middle East within one year of George W. Bush taking office as President of the United States. (We now know how that turned out. It looks as if William Cooper may have been on to something after all.)

9.

On The Life And Death of Bill Cooper By Kenn Thomas

Jim Keith always wanted to be "a hip Bill Cooper," he said to me on several occasions. My own experience told me that there would never be more than one Bill Cooper. My attention was first drawn to him by the title of his book, Behold A Pale Horse, which was also the title of the first draft of Danny Casolaro's Octopus manuscript. Although I didn't share Jim's ambition, I did become fascinated by his unusual outlook and I mourn his passing.

I met Cooper on a couple of occasions at UFO conferences. He was anything but "hip." In fact, he seemed to take great delight in publicly insulting the conferees that had come to hear him speak. They, in turn, could not get enough of the insults. They lined up to attend the workshop following his lecture, which had a separate attendance fee. It contrasted sharply with the half-dozen people who signed up for my modest effort to lecture on the UFO involvements of Wilhelm Reich.

That happened before Cooper changed his mind about the extraterrestrial presence. He was calling people "sheeple" then, not yet labeling them "ufoologists." At the conference I encountered him next, he was urging his fans to buy into billboard advertising and give him their proxy vote in decisions over what gets put on the billboards. His messages would be more anti-NWO than pro-UFO. About UFOs, he later would write, "For many years I sincerely believed that an extraterrestrial threat existed and that it was the most important driving force behind world events. I was wrong and for that I most deeply and humbly apologize."

He never abandoned his basic rant, however. "Many years ago I had access to a set of documents," wrote Cooper, "that I eventually realized was the plan for the destruction of the United States of America and the formation of a socialist totalitarian world government. The plan was contained within a set of Top Secret documents with the title MAJESTYTWELVE." His memories of this were chillingly detailed: "There was no space between majesty and twelve." As I have pointed out elsewhere, credible documentary evidence, involving nobody's misremembered experience, exists that such a group, MJ12, does or did indeed exist.

I clashed with Cooper once in Rob Sterling's Konformist newsletter. He made some disparaging remarks about John Lennon, calling the singer some kind of spokesman for world socialism. I had to point out to him that Lennon actually was a filthy rich, capitalist rock star. At another point, I was happy to pass along a tape of answering machine messages left by Cooper on the machine of someone he believed stole the master video copy of his "Driver Did It" lecture - in which he claimed that William Greer, the driver of JFK's Lincoln on November 22, turned and shot the president with a .45. The answering machine messages were hilarious in that each one reflected Cooper becoming progressively more drunk and ended finally with him threatening to visit the alleged thief to slash the tires of his car.

I even came to Cooper's defense over the JFK thing. A .45 slug was found on Elm Street. The Lincoln's brake lights do come on in the Zapruder film, suggesting that Greer did have some involvement in the conspiracy. True, Cooper was using an atrociously bad copy of the Z-film to "show" that Greer with a gun in his hand. (The full story of the "Driver Did It" theory is found in Lars Hanson's unpublished affidavit on the subject.)

But let's not throw the baby out with the bath water, I argued. At the very least, Bill Cooper created a cartoon version of conspiracy reality that attracted more attention to the serious issues.

Cooper was right in his broad strokes. He certainly was not alone in looking into the political and cultural environment and seeing an evil monster, and he was more articulate than most in getting across what that feels like. Cooper was no doubt right about the IRS being a legal fiction, and fully aware that it's a fiction protected by the brutal reality of police force. He thought it shouldn't be that way. His tax resistance was the concrete expression of opposition to the encroaching forces of oppression-an enemy shared by anti-WTO demonstrators and the militias alike. Unlike many of those weekend warriors, Cooper took the bullet for what he believed in.

Those who have been quick to point out that the shooting death of William Cooper did not arise from the federal indictments against him, but rather from the local police responding to Cooper's dangerous behavior, ignore the close cooperation that exists between local police and federal authorities. But neither group has a monopoly on bad schemes to capture and imprison harmless citizens. Cooper had lost a leg in military service. Feds or no, there were certainly other, non-lethal ways to get Bill Cooper under arrest.

Those who admired Cooper, those who were appalled by him and the rest of us in between cannot help but wonder why his fate seemed inevitable.

10.
My Thoughts on the Late Bill Cooper From Norio Hayakawa

The world will always remember Bill Cooper as an egotistic paranoia monger. Indeed, to many he was an arrogant, obnoxious, choleric, self-aggrandizing, rude, vitriolic and vengeful person.

Perhaps he was all of this and much more. But no matter how negative his personality is described to be, we must admit the fact that he did indeed make a tremendous impact among hundreds, if not, thousands of his listeners, whether in front of his astounded lecture audiences or through his "shocking" radio programs.

I first met Bill back in 1989 in West L.A. when he was just an unknown speaker and where he spoke for the first time at a gathering called UFORUM. I was quite stunned then with his hypothesis on the Secret Government. It really sounded so fresh at that time because unlike most UFO speakers of that time he convincingly injected "UFOs" to a "one-world government" right-wing flavored conspiracy theory. I was so impacted by his hypothesis that I became a volunteer and helped him organize his first successful major public appearance that same year, which was held at Hollywood High School. That became the historic launching pad for his national lecture circuit. And the rest is history.

Later, in December of that year, I even attended the controversial National MUFON Conference held in Las Vegas in which Bill Cooper was perhaps the most controversial speaker aside from John Lear and Bill Moore and others. The Bill Cooper of then was very much into ufology, it seemed. Even in 1991 when Gary Schultz and I organized the first Ultimate Seminar in Rachel, Nevada (25 miles north of Area 51), we were surprised to see Bill Cooper as an attendee. I remember quite well when we lead the people to the White Sides hill for a climb to see the base, Bill Cooper could not make the climb due to his leg and he was even cracking up jokes about it.

In 1993 Bill Cooper, Eustace Mullins, Jordan Maxwell, Vladmir Terziski, Dr. Robert Strecker, Anthony Hilder, a couple of other conspiracy speakers and myself were all invited to speak at the First International Conference on Global Deception to be held in the famous Wembley Arena in London. Because of concerns for security due to the highly controversial nature of the conference and its speakers, the bulk of us decided not to travel to England. Nevertheless, Bill Cooper had the guts to go ahead and speak at the conference. I admired him for that.

WILLIAM COOPER: DEATH OF A CONSPIRACY SALESMAN

By 1993 I had completely abandoned the so-called "extraterrestrial hypothesis" of the origins of the so-called UFO phenomena and began to promote the hypothesis that the entire UFO phenomena was a brilliantly concocted, staged and manipulated man-made deception by elitists to bring about certain agendas. I completely disassociated myself with "ufology."

I was quite surprised to learn that, later on, Bill Cooper also began to depart from "ufology" and was also beginning to hypothesize that the "UFOs" had nothing to do with "aliens" but was a manipulation of the government to bring about fear to create a one-world government. Cooper began to admit that he most likely had been shown disinformation by the government while he was in the service. On this point, I truly commended Cooper for his admission. Cooper began to state that he was not a ufologist. It was Cooper who coined the term "ufoology" and I also commended him for it. However, Cooper had a tendency to label anyone that didn't agree with him as "agents of CIA", etc.

After moving to Arizona, he shifted his focus to the Patriot Movement (the militia movement), although in reality he was just a one-man militia, simply promoting his view on the Constitutional Republic through his radio programs to thousands of listeners.

Besides his other numerous negative traits, Cooper had an uncontrollable alcoholic problem. But despite his eccentric, obnoxious personality, deep in his heart I believe that he wanted to be a good person. Unfortunately he brought an end to his tumultuous life by his self-fulfilled prophecy through his violent act.

My heart goes out to Annie and the children. But my heart goes out just as much to Deputy Marinez, at the young age of 40, who was shot by Cooper and who is still in a critical condition. Even if the Deputy should recover, he will most likely live the rest of his life with brain damage and paralysis. I feel so sorry for the Deputy's wife and his children. Cooper will have to answer to God for his actions, no doubt. May we all learn from this tragedy.

11.
AIDS – Manufactured Disease to Kill-Off Undesirable Population - By William Cooper

During my talks in Las Vegas last weekend, I revealed a few things about aids that I have been keeping close to my chest. I have already revealed that I saw that AIDS was man made to eliminate the undesirable elements of society while I was attached to Naval Security and Intelligence. I stated this fact in my paper "The Secret Government." Now for the rest of the story.

The first study was made in 1957 by scientists meeting in Huntsville Alabama. That study resulted in "Alternative 3." Another study was made by the Club of Rome in 1968 to determine the limits to growth. The result of the study was that civilization as we know it would collapse shortly after the year 2000 unless the population was seriously curtailed. Several Top Secret recommendations were made to the ruling elite by Dr. Aurelio Peccei of the Club of Rome.

The chief recommendation was to develop a microbe which would attack the auto immune system and thus render the development of a vaccine impossible. The orders were given to develop the microbe and to also develop a cure and a prophylactic. The microbe would be used against the general population and would be introduced by vaccine administered by the World Health Organization. The prophylactic was to be used by the ruling elite. The cure will be administered to the survivors when they decide that enough people have died. It will be announced as newly developed. This plan was called Global 2000.

The cure and the prophylactic are suppressed. Funding was obtained from the U.S. Congress under H.B. 15090 where $10 million was given to the Department of Defense to produce, "a synthetic biological agent, an agent that does not naturally exist and for which no natural immunity could have been acquired."

"Within the next 5 to 10 years it would probably be possible to make a new infective microorganism which could differ in certain important aspects from any known disease causing organisms. Most important of these is that it might be refractory to the immunological and therapeutic processes upon which we depend to maintain our relative freedom from infectious disease."

The project was carried out at Fort Detrick Maryland. Since large populations were to be decimated, the ruling elite decided to target the "undesirable elements of society" for extermination. Specifically targeted were the black, Hispanic, and homosexual populations. The name of the project that developed AIDS is MKNAOMI. The African continent was infected via smallpox vaccine in 1977.

The U.S. population was infected in 1978 with the hepatitis B vaccine through the Centers for Disease Control and the New York Blood Center. You now have the entire story. The order was given by the POLICY COMMITTEE of THE BILDERBERG GROUP based in Switzerland. Other measures were also ordered. The one you will be able to check the easiest is the Haig - Kissinger Depopulation Policy which is administered by the State Department.

When you put this information out do not edit it and please give me and this board full credit as the source of the information. Please post the board phone number with this file. That is how I stay alive. This board is THE CITIZENS AGENCY FOR JOINT INTELLIGENCE, SYSOP - WILLIAM COOPER, (602) 567-6725

To aid you in your research of this CRIME the name of the report was "THE LIMITS TO GROWTH" A REPORT FOR THE CLUB OF ROME'S PROJECT ON THE PREDICAMENT OF MANKIND. In April 1968 the study began in the Accademia dei Lincei in Rome Italy. They met at the instigation of Dr. Aurelio Peccei. The Top Secret recommendations of the results of the study were made by Dr. Aurelio Peccei who pledged not to use the prophylactic and not to take the cure should the microbe be developed and should he contract the disease.

Dr. Peccei was hailed as a great hero for deciding to take the same risk as the general population. The public results of the study were published in 1972. The MIT project team that participated in the study are listed below:

Dr. Dennis L. Meadows, director, United States

Dr. Alison A. Anderson, United States (pollution)

Dr. Jay M. Anderson, United States (pollution)

Ilyas Bayar, Turkey (agriculture)

WILLIAM COOPER: DEATH OF A CONSPIRACY SALESMAN

William W. Behrens III, United States (resources)

Farhad Hakimzadeh, Iran (population)

Dr. Steffen Harbordt, Germany (socio-political trends)

Judith A Machen, United States (administration)

Dr. Donella H. Meadows, United States (population)

Peter Milling, Germany (capital)

Nirmala S. Murthy, India (population)

Roger F. Naill, United States (resources)

Jorgen Randers, Norway (population)

Stephen Shantzis, United States (agriculture)

John A. Seeger, United States (administration)

Marilyn Williams, United States (documentation)

Dr. Erich K. O. Zahn, Germany (agriculture)

When the study was completed in 1969, U.N. Secretary General U Thant made this statement:

"I do not wish to seem overdramatic, but I can only conclude from the information that is available to me as Secretary-General, that the Members of the United Nations have perhaps ten years left in which to subordinate their ancient quarrels and launch a global partnership to curb the arms race, to defuse the population explosion, and to supply the required momentum to development efforts. If such a global partnership is not forged within the next decade, then I very much fear that the problems I have mentioned will have reached such staggering proportions that they will be beyond our capacity to control."

MKNAOMI was developed by the Special Operations Division (SOD) scientists at Ft. Detrick, Maryland under the supervision of the CIA and for the CIA. A reference to the project MKNAOMI can be found in Fain, Tyrus G., and Katharine C. Plant. "The Intelligence Community: History, Organization, and Issues." New York: R. R. Bowker, 1977.

I swear that all of the above information is true and correct to the best of my memory and knowledge. I give this information to the people of the world in hopes that someone will have the courage and resources to help me end this madness. The illuminati (the order) are in complete control of most of the world and they have declared war against the general populations of all nations. We must stop them at all costs.

(Authors Note) William Cooper was not alone in his belief that AIDS is a man-made disease. Alan Cantwell, Jr, MD stated that, "Since the beginning of the AIDS epidemic there have been persistent rumors that the disease was man-made, and that HIV was deliberately "introduced" into the American gay and the African black populations as a germ warfare experiment. This so-called conspiracy theory was quickly squelched by virologists and molecular biologists, who blamed primates in the African bush and human sexuality for the introduction and spread of HIV.

"Lost in the history of AIDS is evidence pointing to HIV as a virus whose origin traces back to animal cancer retrovirus experimentation in the "pre-AIDS" years of the 1960s and 70s. Evidence linking the introduction of HIV into gays and blacks via vaccine experiments and programs in the late 1970s has been totally ignored."

12.

Operation Majority – Final Release
By William Cooper

I Milton William Cooper, 1311 S. Highland #205, Fullerton, California, 92632, (714) 680-9537, do solemnly swear that the information contained in this file is true to the best of my knowledge. I swear I saw this information in 1972 in the performance of my duties as a member of the Intelligence Briefing Team of the Commander in Chief of the Pacific Fleet as a Petty Officer in the US Navy.

I swear that I can and will take a lie detector test or any other test of any reputable persons choosing in order to confirm this information. I swear that I can and will undergo hypnotic regression conducted by any reputable and qualified Doctor of any reputable persons choosing in order to confirm this information. I will not, however submit to any test or hypnosis by anyone who is now or has ever been connected with the Government in any capacity for obvious reasons.

The following is a brief listing of everything that I personally saw and know from 1972 and does not contain input from any other source whatsoever.

MAJESTY was listed as the code word for the President of the United States for communications concerning this information.

OPERATION MAJORITY is the name of the operation responsible for every aspect, project, and consequence of alien presence on earth.

GRUDGE Contains 16 volumes of documented information collected from the beginning of the United States investigation of Unidentified Flying Objects (UFO's) and Identified Alien Crafts (IAC). The project was funded by CIA confidential funds (non-appropriated) and money from the illicit drug trade. Participation in the illegal drug trade was justified in that it would identify and eliminate the weak elements of our society. The purpose of project GRUDGE was to collect all scientific, technological, medical and intelligence information from UFO/IAC sightings and contacts with alien life forms. This orderly file of collected information has been used to advance the United States Space Program.

WILLIAM COOPER: DEATH OF A CONSPIRACY SALESMAN

MJ-12 is the name of the secret control group. President Eisenhower commissioned a secret society known as THE JASON SOCIETY (JASON SCHOLARS) to sift through all the facts, evidence, technology, lies and deception and find the truth of the alien question. The society was made up of 32 most prominent men in the country in 1972 and the top 12 members were designated MJ-12. MJ-12 has total control of everything. They are designated by the code J-1, J-2, J-3, etc. all the way through the members of the Jason Society. The director of the CIA is appointed J-1 and is the director of MJ-12. MJ-12 is only responsible to the President.

MJ-12 runs most of the world's illegal drug trade. This was done to hide funding and thus keep the secret from Congress and the people of the United States. It was justified in that it would identify and eliminate the weak elements of our society. The cost of funding the alien connected projects is higher than anything you can imagine. MJ-12 assassinated President Kennedy when he informed them that he was going to tell the public all the facts of the alien presence.

The Secret Service agent driving his car killed him and it is plainly visible in the film held from public view. A secret meeting place was built for MJ-12 in MARYLAND and it was described as only accessible by air. It contains full living, recreational, and other facilities for MJ-12 and the JASON SOCIETY. It is code named "THE COUNTRY CLUB". Only those with TOP SECRET/MAJIC clearance are allowed to go there.

MAJI is the MAJORITY AGENCY FOR JOINT INTELLIGENCE. All information, disinformation, and intelligence is gathered and evaluated by this agency. The agency is responsible for all disinformation and operates in conjunction with the CIA, NSA, and the Defense Intelligence Agency. This is a very powerful organization and all alien projects are under its control. MAJI is only responsible to MJ-12.

SIGMA is the project which first established communications with the aliens and is still responsible for communications.

PLATO is the project responsible for Diplomatic relations with the aliens. This project secured a formal treaty (illegal under the Constitution) with the aliens. The terms were that the aliens would give us technology. In return, we agreed to keep their presence on earth a secret, not to interfere in any way their actions, and to allow them to abduct humans and animals. The aliens agreed to furnish MJ-12 with a list of abductees on a periodic basis.

MAJIC is a security classification and clearance of all alien connected material, projects, and information. MAJIC means MAJI controlled.

AQUARIUS is a project which compiled the history of alien presence and their interaction with Homo Sapiens upon this planet for the last 25,000 years and culminating with the Basque people who live in the mountainous country on the border of France and Spain and the Syrians.

GARNET is the project responsible for control of all information and documents regarding this subject and accountability of the information and documents.

PLUTO is a project to evaluate all UFO/IAC information pertaining to space technology.

POUNCE is the project formed to recover all downed/crashed craft and aliens.

REDLIGHT is the project to test fly recovered alien craft. It is conducted at AREA 51 (DREAMLAND) in Nevada. It was aided when the aliens gave us craft and helped us fly them. The initial project was somewhat successful in that we flew a recovered craft but it blew up in the air and the pilots were killed. The project was suspended at that time until the aliens agreed to help us.

SNOWBIRD was established as a cover for project REDLIGHT. Several flying saucer type craft were built using conventional technology. They were unveiled to the press and flown in front of the press. The purpose was to explain accidental sightings or disclosure of REDLIGHT as having been SNOWBIRD craft.

LUNA is the alien base on the far side of the Moon. It was seen and filmed by Apollo Astronauts. A base, a mining operation using very large machines, and a very large alien craft described in sighting reports as MOTHER SHIPS exist there.

NRO is the National Recon Organization based at Fort Carson, Colorado. It is responsible for security for all alien or alien craft connected projects.

DELTA is the designation for the specific arm of the NRO which is especially trained and tasked with security of these projects.

JOSHUA is a project to develop a low frequency pulsed sound generating weapon. It is said that this weapon would be effective against the alien craft and beam weapons.

EXCALIBUR is a weapon to destroy the alien underground bases. It is a missile capable of penetrating 1000 meters of Tufa/hard packed soil such as that found in New Mexico with no operational damage. Missile apogee not to exceed 30,000 feet AGL and impact must not deviate in excess of 50 meters from designated target. The device will carry a 1 megaton nuclear warhead.

ALIENS, there were 4 types of aliens mentioned in the papers. A LARGE NOSED GREY with whom we have the treaty, the GREY reported in abductee cases that works for the LARGE NOSED GREY, a blond human like type described as NORDIC, a red haired human like type called ORANGE. The home of the aliens were described as being a star in the constellation of Orion, Barnards star, and Zeta Riticuli 1 and 2. I cannot remember even under hypnosis which alien belongs to which star.

EBE is the name or designation given to the live alien captured at the 1949 Roswell crash. He died in captivity.

KRLL OR KRLLL OR CRLL OR CRLLL pronounced Crill or Krill was the hostage left with us at the first Holloman landing as a pledge that the aliens would carry out their part of the basic agreement that was reached during that meeting. KRLL gave us the foundation of the yellow book which was completed by the guests at a later date. KRLL became sick and was nursed by Dr. G. Mendoza who became an expert in alien biology and medicine. KRLL later died. His information was disseminated under the pseudonym O.H. Cril or Crill.

GUESTS were aliens exchanged for humans who gave us the balance of the yellow book. At the time I saw the information there were only 3 left alive. They were called (ALF's) Alien Life Forms.

RELIGION The aliens claim to have created Homo Sapiens through hybridization. The papers said the RH-blood was proof of this. They further claim to have created all our major religions. The showed a Hologram of the crucifixion of Christ which the Government filmed. They claim Jesus was created by them.

ALIEN BASES exist in the four corners area of Utah, Colorado, New Mexico, and Nevada. Six bases were described in the 1972 papers, all on Indian reservations and all in the Four Corners area. The base near Dulce was one of them.

MURDER The documents stated that many military and government personnel had been terminated (murdered without due process of law) when they attempted to reveal the secret.

CRAFT RECOVERY'S. The documents stated that many craft had been recovered. The early ones from Roswell, Aztec, Roswell again, Texas, Mexico, and other places.

GENERAL DOOLITTLE made a prediction that one day we would have to reckon with the aliens and the document stated that it appeared that General Doolittle was correct.

ABDUCTIONS were occurring long before 1972.

The document stated that humans and or animals were being abducted and or mutilated. Many vanished without a trace. They were taking sperm and ova samples, tissue, performed surgical operations, implanted a spherical device 40 to 80 microns in size near the optic nerve in the brain and all attempts to remove it resulted in the death of the patient. The document estimated that 1 out of every 40 people had been implanted. This implant was said to give the aliens total control of that human.

CONTINGENCY PLAN SHOULD THE INFORMATION BECOME PUBLIC OR SHOULD THE ALIENS ATTEMPT TAKEOVER

This plan called for a public announcement that a terrorist group had entered the United States with an Atomic weapon. It would be announced that the terrorists planned to detonate the weapon in a major city. Martial law would be declared and all persons with implants would be rounded up along with all dissidents and would be placed in concentration camps. The press, radio, and TV would be nationalized and controlled. Anyone attempting to resist would be arrested or killed.

CONTINGENCY PLAN TO CONTAIN OR DELAY RELEASE OF INFORMATION

This plan called for the use of MAJESTIC TWELVE as a disinformation ploy to delay and confuse the release of information should anyone get close to the truth. It was selected because of its similarity to MJ-12. It was designed to confuse memory and to result is a fruitless search for material which did not exist.

SOURCE OF THE MATERIAL CONTAINED IN THE DOCUMENTS WHICH I SAW

The source of the material was an ONI counter intelligence operation against MJ-12 in order for the Navy to find out the truth of what was really going on. The Navy (at that time or at least the Navy that I worked for) were not participants in any of this. The different services and the government conduct this type of operation against each other all the time. The result of this operation was that the Navy cut themselves in for a piece of the action (technology) and control of some projects.

HISTORY WILL BE THE JUDGE OF ME AND THIS INFORMATION AND I HAVE NO FEAR OF THAT JUDGMENT. I SWEAR THAT THIS INFORMATION IS TRUE AND CORRECT TO THE BEST OF MY KNOWLEDGE.

I wish to thank all those people who have aided me in reaching this point and for their patience and understanding. I owe you all more than I can ever repay.

Finally, it does not matter who is right or who is wrong or if a project name is in the wrong place. It does not matter who is working for who or what is really what. It should be obvious that something sinister and terribly wrong is going on involving the government and the UFO phenomenon. We must all band together and expose it now. I have done my part in the best way that I could. I can add nothing else except my testimony in Congress or a court of law that what I saw and have written in this file is true and that I saw it.

13.
The Origin, Identity and Purpose of MJ-12
By William Cooper

During the years following World War II, the government of the United States was confronted with a series of events which were to change beyond prediction its future and with it the future of humanity. These events were so incredible that they defied belief. A stunned President Truman and his top military Commanders found themselves virtually impotent after having just won the most devastating and costly war in history.

The United States had developed, used, and was the only nation on earth in possession of the Atomic Bomb which alone had the potential to destroy any enemy, and even the Earth itself. At that time the United States had the best economy, the most advanced technology, the highest standard of living, exerted the most influence, and fielded the largest and most powerful military forces in history. We can only imagine the confusion and concern when the informed elite of the United States Government discovered that an alien spacecraft piloted by insect-like beings from a totally incomprehensible culture had crashed in the desert of New Mexico.

Between January 1947 and December 1952 at least 16 crashed or downed alien craft, 65 alien bodies, and 1 live alien were recovered. An additional alien craft had exploded and nothing was recovered from that incident. Of these incidents, 13 occurred within the borders of the United States not including the craft which disintegrated in the air. Of these 13, 1 was in Arizona, 11 were in New Mexico, and 1 was in Nevada.

Three occurred in foreign countries. Of those 1 was in Norway, and the last 2 were in Mexico. Sightings of UFO's were so numerous that serious investigation and debunking of each report became impossible utilizing the existing intelligence assets.

Alien-Earth Presence

An alien craft was found on February 13, 1948 on a mesa near Aztec, New Mexico. Another craft was located on March 25, 1948 in Hart Canyon near Aztec, New Mexico. It was 100 feet in diameter. A total of 17 alien bodies were recovered from those two craft. Of even greater significance was the discovery of a large number of human body parts stored within both of these vehicles. A demon had reared its ugly head and paranoia quickly took hold of everyone then "in the know."

The secret lid immediately became an Above Top Secret lid and was screwed down tight. The security blanket was even tighter than that imposed upon the Manhattan Project. In the coming years these events were to become the most closely guarded secrets in the history of the world.

A special group of America's top scientists were organized and a program under the name Project Sign was created in December of 1947 to study the phenomenon. The whole nasty business was contained within the shroud of secrecy. Project Sign evolved into Project Grudge in December of 1948.

A low level collection and disinformation project named Blue Book was formed under Grudge. 16 volumes were to come out of Grudge including the controversial "Grudge 13" which I and Bill English saw, read, and revealed to the public. "Blue Teams" were put together to recover the crashed disks and dead or alive aliens. The Blue Teams were later to evolve into Alpha Teams under Project Pounce.

During these early years the United States Air Force and the CIA exercised complete control over the Alien Secret. In fact the CIA was formed by Presidential Executive Order first as the Central Intelligence Group for the express purpose of dealing with the alien presence.

Later the National Security Act (NSA) was established to oversee the intelligence community and especially the alien endeavor. A series of National Security Council memos and Executive Orders removed the CIA from the sole task of gathering foreign intelligence and slowly but thoroughly "legalized" direct action in the form of covert activities at home and abroad.

Intelligence Gathering
On December 9, 1947, Truman approved issuance of NSC-4, entitled "Coordination of Foreign Intelligence Information Measures" at the urging of Secretaries Marshall, Forrestal, Patterson, and the director of the State Department's Policy Planning Staff, Kennan.

The Foreign and Military Intelligence, Book 1, "Final Report of the Select Committee to Study Governmental operations with respect to Intelligence Activities.", United States Senate, 94th Congress, 2nd Session, Report No. 94-

755, April 26, 1976, page 49 states: "This directive empowered the secretary of state to coordinate overseas information activities designed to counter communism."

A top secret annex to NSC-4, NSC-4A, instructed the director of Central Intelligence to undertake covert psychological activities in pursuit of the aims set forth in NSC-4. The initial authority given the CIA for covert operations under NSC-4A did not establish formal procedures for either coordinating or approving these operations. It simply directed the DCI to "undertake covert actions and ensure, through liaison with State and Defense, that the resulting operations were consistent with American policy."

Later NSC-10/1 and NSC-10/2 were to supersede NSC-4 and NSC-4A and expand the covert abilities even further. The Office of Policy Coordination (OPC) was chartered to carry out an expanded program of covert activities. NSC-10/1 and NSC-10/2 validated illegal and extra-legal practices and procedures as being agreeable to the national security leadership. The reaction was swift. In the eyes of the intelligence community "no holes were barred".

Under NSC-10/1 an Executive Coordination Group, was established to review, but not approve, covert project proposals. The CG was secretly tasked to coordinate the alien projects. NSC-10/1 and NSC-10/2 were interpreted to mean that no one at the top wanted to know about anything until it was over and successful. These actions established a buffer between the President and the information. It was intended that this buffer serve as a means for the President to deny knowledge if leaks divulged the true state of affairs.

This buffer was used in later years for the purpose of effectively isolating succeeding Presidents from the knowledge of the alien presence other than what the Secret Government and the intelligence community wanted them to know. NSC-10/2 established a study panel which met secretly and was made up of scientific minds of the day. The study panel was NOT called MJ-12. Another NSC memo, NSC-10/5 further outlined the duties of the study panel. These NSC memos and secret Executive Orders set the stage for the creation of MJ-12 only 4 years later.

First Victim of the Cover-up

Secretary of defense James Forrestal began to object to the secrecy. He was a very idealistic and religious man who believed that the public should be told. When he began to talk to leaders of the opposition party and leaders of congress about the alien problem he was asked to resign by Truman. He expressed his fears to many people and rightfully believed that he was being watched. This was interpreted by those who were ignorant of the facts as paranoia.

Forrestal later was said to have suffered a mental breakdown and was admitted to Bethesda Naval Hospital. In fact it was feared that Forrestal would begin to talk again and he had to be isolated and discredited. Sometime in the early morning of May 22, 1949 agents of the CIA tied a sheet around his neck, fastened the other end to a fixture in his room and threw James Forrestal out the window.

The sheet tore and he plummeted to his death. He became one of the first victims of the cover-up.

EBE

The live alien that had been taken from the 1947 Roswell crash was named EBE. The name had been suggested by Dr. Vannever Bush and was short for Extraterrestrial Biological Entity. EBE had a tendency to lie and for over a year would give only the desired answer to questions asked. Those questions which would have resulted in an undesirable answer went unanswered.

At some point during the second year of captivity he began to open up and the information derived from EBE was startling, to say the least. This compilation of his revelations became the foundation of what would later be called the "Yellow Book". Photographs were taken of EBE which, among others, I and Bill English were to view years later in GRUDGE 13. In late 1951 EBE became ill. Medical personnel had been unable to determine the cause of EBE's illness and had no background from which to draw.

EBE's system was chlorophyll based and he processed food into energy much the same as plants. Waste material was excreted the same as plants. It was decided that an expert on botany was called for. A botanist, Dr. Guillermo Mendoza, was brought in to try and help him recover. Dr. Mendoza worked to save EBE until mid-1952 when EBE died. Dr. Mendoza became an expert on alien biology.

In a futile attempt to save EBE and to gain favor with this technologically superior alien race the United States began broadcasting a call for help early in

1952 into the vast regions of space. The call went unanswered but the project continued as an effort of good faith.

Creation of the NSA

President Truman created the super secret National Security Agency (NSA) by secret Executive Order on November 4, 1952. Its primary purpose was to decipher the alien communications and language and establish a dialogue with the aliens. This most urgent task was a continuation of the earlier effort and was code named SIGMA.

The secondary purpose of the NSA was to monitor all communications and emissions from any and all devices worldwide for the purpose of gathering intelligence, both human and alien, and to contain the secret of the alien presence.

Project SIGMA was successful. The NSA also maintains communications with the Luna base and other secret space programs. By Executive Order the NSA is exempt from all laws which do not specifically name the NSA in the text of the law as being subject to that law. That means that if the agency is not spelled out in the text of any and every law passed by the Congress it is not subject to that or those laws. The NSA now performs many other duties and in fact is the premiere agency within the intelligence community.

Today NSA receives 75% of the moneys allotted to the intelligence community. The old saying, "Where the money goes therein the power resides" is true. The DCI today is a figure head maintained as a public ruse. The primary task of the NSA is still alien communications but now includes other Alien projects as well.

President Truman had been keeping our allies, including the Soviet Union, informed of the developing alien problem since the Roswell recovery. This had been done in case the aliens turned out to be a threat to the human race. Plans were formulated to defend the Earth in case of invasion.

Great difficulty was encountered in maintaining international secrecy. It was decided that an outside group was necessary to coordinate and control international efforts in order to hide the secret from the normal scrutiny of governments by the press. The result was the formation of a secret society known as the "Bilderbergers," better known as the "Bilderberg Group" The headquarters of this group is in Geneva, Switzerland.

The Bilderbergers evolved into a secret world government that now controls everything. The United Nations was then, and is now, an international joke.

A New President

In 1953, a new man occupied the White House. He was a man used to a structured staff organization with a chain of command. His method was to delegate authority and rule by committee. He made major decisions but only when his advisors were unable to come to consensus. His normal method was to read through or listen to several alternatives and then approve one.

Those who worked closely with him have stated that his favorite comment was, "just do whatever it takes". He spent a lot of time on the golf course. This was not all unusual for a man who had been career Army with the ultimate position of Supreme Allied Commander during the war. A post which carried 5 stars along with it. This president was General of the Army Dwight David Eisenhower.

During his first year in office, 1953, at least 10 more alien crashed disks were recovered along with 26 dead and 4 live aliens. Of the 10, 4 were found in Arizona, 2 in Texas, 1 in New Mexico, 1 in Louisiana, 1 in Montana, and 1 in South Africa. There were hundreds of sightings.

Eisenhower knew that he had to wrestle and beat the alien problem. He knew that he could not do it by revealing the secret to the Congress. Early in 1953 the new president turned to his friend and fellow member of the Council on Foreign Relations, Nelson Rockefeller for help with the alien problem.

Eisenhower and Rockefeller began planning the secret structure of alien task supervision which was to become a reality within one year. The idea for MJ-12 was thus born. It was Nelson's Uncle Winthrop Aldrich who had been crucial in convincing Eisenhower to run for President.

The whole Rockefeller family and with them the Rockefeller empire had solidly backed Ike. Asking Rockefeller for help with the alien problem was to be the biggest mistake Eisenhower ever made for the future of the United States and most probably all of humanity.

Within 1 week of Eisenhower's election he had appointed Nelson Rockefeller chairman of a Presidential Advisory Committee on Government Organization. Rockefeller was responsible for planning the reorganization of the government. New Deal programs went into 1 single cabinet position called the Department of Health, Education, and Welfare. When the Congress approved the new cabinet position in April of 1953, Nelson was named to the post of Undersecretary to Oveta Culp Hobby.

Heading For Earth

In 1953 astronomers discovered large objects in space which were moving towards Earth. It was first believed that they were asteroids. Later evidence proved that the objects could only be spaceships. Project Sigma intercepted alien radio communication. When the objects reached the Earth they took up a very high orbit around the equator. There were several huge ships, and their actual intent was unknown.

Project Sigma, and a new project, Plato, through radio communications using the computer binary language, was able to arrange a landing that resulted in face to face contact with alien beings from another planet. Project Plato was tasked with establishing diplomatic relations with this alien race of space aliens.

In the meantime, a race of human-looking aliens contacted the U.S. Government. This alien group warned us against the aliens that were orbiting the Equator and offered to help us with our spiritual development.

They demanded that we dismantle and destroy our nuclear weapons as the major condition. They refused to exchange technology citing that we were spiritually unable to handle the technology which we then possessed. They believed that we would use any new technology to destroy each other. This race stated that we were on a path of self-destruction and we must stop killing each other, stop polluting the earth, stop raping the Earth's natural resources, and learn to live in harmony.

These terms were met with extreme suspicion especially the major condition of nuclear disarmament. It was believed that meeting that condition would leave us helpless in the face of an obvious alien threat. We also had nothing in history to help with the decision. Nuclear disarmament was not considered to be within the best interest of the United States. The overtures were rejected.

Later in 1954 the race of large nosed gray aliens which had been orbiting the Earth landed at Holloman Air Force base. A basic agreement was reached. This race identified themselves as originating from a planet around a red star in the Constellation of Orion which we call Betelgeuse. They stated that their home planet was dying and that at some unknown future time they would not be able to survive there. This led to a second landing at Edwards Air Force base.

The historical event had been planned in advance and details of the treaty had been agreed upon. Eisenhower arranged to be in Palm Springs on vacation. On the appointed day, the President was spirited away to the base and the excuse was given to the press that he was visiting a dentist.

Formal Treaty Signed

President Eisenhower met with the aliens and a formal treaty between the alien nation and the United States of America was signed. We then received our first alien ambassador from outer space. His name and title was his "Omnipotent Highness Krlll", pronounced Krill.

In the American tradition of disdain for royal titles, he was secretly called "Original Hostage Krlll". You should know that the alien flag is known as the "Trilateral Insignia". It is displayed on their craft and worn on their uniforms. Both of these landings and the second meeting were filmed. The films exist today.

The treaty stated: The aliens would not interfere in our affairs and we would not interfere in theirs. We would keep their presence on Earth a secret. They would furnish us with advanced technology and would help us in our technological development. They would not make any treaty with any other earth nation.

They could abduct humans on a limited and periodic basis for the purpose of medical examination and monitoring of our development with the stipulation that the humans would not be harmed, would be returned to their point of abduction, that the humans would have no memory of the event, and that the alien nation would furnish MJ-12 a list of all human contacts and abductees on a regularly scheduled basis.

It was agreed that each nation would receive the ambassador of the other for as long as the treaty remained in force. It was further agreed that the alien nation and the United States would exchange 16 personnel each to the other with the purpose of learning, each of the other.

Underground Bases

The alien "guests" would remain on Earth and the "human guests" would travel to the alien point of origin for a specified period of time then return, at which point a reverse exchange would be made. It was also agreed that bases would be constructed underground for the use of the alien nation and that 2 bases would be constructed for the joint use of the alien nation and the United States government.

Exchange of technology would take place in the jointly occupied bases. These alien bases would be constructed under Indian reservations in the four corners area of Utah, New Mexico, Arizona, and Colorado, and one would be constructed in Nevada in the area known as S-4 located approximately 7 miles south of the western border of Area 51.

All alien bases are under complete control of the Department of Naval Intelligence and all personnel who work in these complexes receive their checks from the Navy. Construction of the bases began immediately but progress was slow until large amounts of money were made available in 1957. Work continued on the "Yellow Book".

Area 51 and S-4

Project REDLIGHT was formed and experimentation in test flying alien aircraft was begun in earnest. A super top-secret facility was built at Groom Lake in Nevada in the midst of the weapons test range. It was code named DREAMLAND. The installation was placed under the Department of the Navy and clearance of all personnel required "Q" clearance as well as Executive (Presidential) approval.

This is ironic due to the fact that the President of the United States does not have clearance to visit the site. The alien base and exchange of technology actually took place in an area known as S-4. Area S-4 was code named "The Dark Side of the Moon".

The Army was tasked to form a super secret organization to furnish security for all alien tasked projects. This organization became the National Reconnaissance Organization based at Fort Carson, Colorado. The specific teams trained to secure the projects were called DELTA.

A second project code named SNOWBIRD was promulgated to explain away any sightings of the REDLIGHT crafts as being Air Force experiments. The

SNOWBIRD crafts were manufactured using conventional technology and were flown for the press on several occasions. Project SNOWBIRD was also used to debunk legitimate public sightings of alien craft (UFO's). Project SNOWBIRD was very successful and reports from the public decline steadily until recent years.

Secret Funding

A multi-million dollar secret fund was organized and kept by the Military Office of the White House. This fund was used to build over 75 deep underground facilities. Presidents who asked were told the fund was used to build deep underground shelters for the President in case of war.

Only a few were built for the President. Millions of dollars were funneled through this office to MJ-12 and then out to the contractors and was used to build top-secret alien bases as well as top-secret DUMB (Deep Underground Military Bases), and facilities promulgated by "Alternative 2", throughout the nation. President Johnson used this fund to build a movie theatre and pave the road on his ranch. He had no idea of its purpose.

The secret White House Underground Construction fund was set up in 1957 by President Eisenhower. The funding was obtained from Congress under the guise of, "construction and maintenance of secret sites where the President could be taken in case of military attack: Presidential Emergency Sites".

The sites are literally holes in the ground, deep enough to withstand a nuclear blast and are out fitted with state of the art communications equipment. To date there are more than seventy five sites spread around the country which were built using money from this fund. The Atomic Energy Commission has built at least an additional 22 underground sites.

The location and everything to do with these sites were and are considered and treated as top-secret. The money was and is in control of the Military Office of the White House, and was and is laundered through a circuitous web that even the most knowledgeable spy or accountant can not follow. As of 1980 only a few at the beginning and end of this web knew what the money was for.

At the beginning were Representative George Mahon, of Texas, and the chairman of the House Appropriations Committee and of its Defense Subcommittee: and Representative Robert Sikes, of Florida, chairman of the House Appropriations Military Construction Subcommittee. Today it is rumored that House Speaker Jim Wright controls the money in Congress and that a power struggle is underway to remove him. At the end of the line were the President, MJ-12, the director of the Military Office and a commander at the Washington Navy Yard.

The money was authorized by the Appropriation Committee who allocated it to the Department of Defense as a top-secret item in the army construction program. The Army, however, could not spend it and in fact did not even know what it was for. Authorization to spend the money was in reality given to the Navy.

The money was channeled to the Chesapeake Division of the Navy Engineers who did not know what it was for either. Not even the Commanding Officer, who was an Admiral, knew what the fund was to be used for. Only one man, a Navy Commander, who was assigned to the Chesapeake Division but in reality was responsible only to the Military Office of the White House knew of the actual purpose, amount, and ultimate destination of the top-secret fund.

The total secrecy surrounding the fund meant that almost every trace of it could be made to disappear by the very few people who controlled it. There has never been and most likely never will be an audit of this secret money.

Large amounts of money were transferred from the top-secret fund to a location at Palm Beach, Florida that belongs to the Coast Guard called Peanut Island. The island is adjacent to property which was owned by Joseph Kennedy. The money was said to have been used for landscaping and general beautification.

Some time ago a TV news special on the Kennedy assassination told of a Coast Guard Officer transferring money in a briefcase to a Kennedy employee across this property line. Could this have been a secret payment to the Kennedy family for the loss of their son John F. Kennedy? The payments continued through the year 1967 and then stopped. The total amount transferred is unknown and the actual use of the money is unknown.

Meanwhile, Nelson Rockefeller changed positions again. This time he was to take C.D. Jackson's old position which had been called the Special Assistant for Psychological Strategy. With Nelson's appointment the name was changed to the Special Assistant for Cold War Strategy.

This position would evolve over the years into the same position Henry Kissinger was ultimately to hold under President Nixon. Officially he was to give "Advice and assistance in development of increased understanding and cooperation among all peoples".

The official description was a smoke screen for security he was the Presidential Coordinator for the Intelligence Community. In his new post, Rockefeller reported directly, and only, to the President. He attended meetings of the Cabinet, the Council on Foreign Economic Policy, and the National Security Council which was the highest policy-making body in the government.

Nelson Rockefeller was also given a second important job as the head of a secret unit called the Planning Coordination Group which was formed under NSC 5412/1 in March of 1955. The group consisted of different ad hoc members depending on the subject of the agenda. The basic members were Rockefeller, a representative of the Department of State, and the Director of Central Intelligence.

It was soon called the "3412 Committee" of the "Special Group". NSC 5412/1 established the rule that covert operations were subject to approval by an executive committee, whereas in the past these operations were initiated solely on the authority of the Director of Central Intelligence.

Founding of MJ-12

By secret Executive Memorandum, NSC 5410, Eisenhower had preceded NSC 5412/1 in 1954 to establish a permanent committee (not ad hoc) to be known as Majority Twelve (MJ-12) to oversee and conduct all covert activities concerned with the alien question. NSC 5412/1 was created to explain the purpose of these meetings when Congress and the Press became curious.

Majority Twelve was made up of: Nelson Rockefeller; the director of the CIA Allen Welsh Dulles; the Secretary of State John Foster Dulles; the Secretary of Defense Charles E.Wilson; the Chairman of the Joint Chiefs of Staff Admiral Arthur W. Radford; the Director of the FBI J. Edgar Hoover; six men from the executive committee of the Council on Foreign Relations known as the "Wise Men."

WILLIAM COOPER: DEATH OF A CONSPIRACY SALESMAN

These men were all members of a secret society of scholars that called themselves "The Jason Society", or "The Jason Scholars" who recruited their members from the "Skull and Bones" and the "Scroll and Key" societies of Harvard and Yale.

The "Wise Men" were key members of the Council on Foreign Relations. There were 12 members including the first 6 from government positions thus Majority Twelve. This group was made up over the years of the top officers and directors of the Council on Foreign Relations and later the Trilateral Commission. Gordon Dean, George Bush, and Zbigniew Brzezinski were among them.

The most important and influential of the "Wise Men" who served on MJ-12 were: John McCloy; Robert Lovett; Averell Harriman; Charles Bohlen; George Kennan; Dean Acheson.

It is significant that President Eisenhower as well as the first six MJ-12 members from the government were also members of the Council on Foreign Relations.

Thorough researchers will soon discover that not all of the "Wise Men" attended Harvard or Yale and not all of them were chosen for "Skull and Bones" or "Scroll and Key" membership during their college years. You will be able to quickly clear up this mystery by obtaining the book "*The Wise Men*" by Walter Issacson and Even Thomas.

Under illustration #9 in the center of the book you will find the caption, "Lovett with the Yale Unit, above far right, and on the beach his initiation into Skull and Bones came at an air base near Dunkirk".

I have found that members were chosen on an ongoing basis by invitation based upon merit post college and was not confined to only Harvard or Yale attendees.

A chosen few were later initiated into the Jason Society. They are all members of the Council on Foreign Relations and at that time were known as the "Eastern Establishment". This should give you a clue to the far reaching and serious nature of these most secret college societies.

WILLIAM COOPER: DEATH OF A CONSPIRACY SALESMAN

The Jason Society is alive and well today but now includes members of the Trilateral Commission as well. The Trilateralists existed secretly several years BEFORE 1973. The name of the Trilateral Commission was taken from the alien flag known as the "Trilateral Insignia."

Majority Twelve was to survive right up to the present day. Under Eisenhower and Kennedy it was erroneously called the "8412 Committee" or more correctly, the "Special Group."

In the Johnson administration it became the "303 Committee" because the name 5412 had been compromised in the book "The Secret Government", actually NSC 5412/1 was leaked to the author to hide existence of NSC 5410. Under Nixon, Ford, and Carter it was called the "40 Committee." Under Reagan, it became the "PI-40 Committee." Over all those years only the name changed.

Deception and Mutilations

By 1955, it became obvious the aliens had deceived Eisenhower and had broken the treaty. Mutilated humans were being found along with mutilated animals all across the United States. It was suspected that the aliens were not submitting a complete list of human contacts and abductees to MJ-12 and it was suspected that not all abductees had been returned. The Soviet Union was suspected of interacting with them and this proved to be true.

It was learned that the aliens had been and were then manipulating masses of people through secret societies, witchcraft, magic, the occult, and religion. After several Air Force combat air engagements with alien craft, it also became apparent that our weapons were no match against them.

In November 1955, NSC 5412/2 was issued establishing a study committee to explore "All factors which are involved in making and implementing of foreign policy in the nuclear age." This was only a blanket of snow that covered the real subject of study, the alien question.

The Study Group

By secret Executive Memorandum, NSC 5411 in 1954, President Eisenhower had commissioned the study group to "examine all the facts, evidence, lies, and deception and discover the truth of the alien question."

WILLIAM COOPER: DEATH OF A CONSPIRACY SALESMAN

NSC5412/2 was only a cover that had become necessary when the press began inquiring as to the purpose of regular meetings of such important men.

The first meetings began at Quantico Marine Base. The study group was made up of 35 members of the Council on Foreign Relations. Secret scholars known as "The Jason Society" of the "Jason Scholars." Dr. Edward Teller was invited to participate. Dr. Zbigniew Brzezinski was the study director for the first 18 months. Dr. Henry Kissinger was chosen as the group's study director for the second 18 months. Nelson Rockefeller was a frequent visitor during the study.

STUDY GROUP MEMBERS

Gordon Dean, Chairman

Dr. Zbigniew Brzezinski, Study Director - 1st phase

Henry Kissinger, Study Director - 2nd phase

Dr. Edward Teller

Maj. Gen. Richard C. Lindsay

Hanson W. Baldwin

Lloyd V. Berkner

Frank C.Nash

Paul H. Nitze

Charles P. Noyes

Frank Pace, Jr.

James A. Perkins

Don K. Price

David Rockefeller

WILLIAM COOPER: DEATH OF A CONSPIRACY SALESMAN

Oscar M. Ruebhausen

Lt. Gen. James M. Gavin

Caryl P. Haskins

James T. Hill, Jr.

Joseph E. Johnson Mervin J. Kelly

Frank Altschul

Hamilton Fish Armstrong

Maj.Gen.James

McCormack, Jr.

Robert R. Bowie

McGeorge Bundy

William A.M. Burden

John C. Campbell

Thomas K. Finletter

George S. Franklin, Jr

I. I. Rabi

Roswell L. Gilpatrio

N. E. Halaby

Gen. Walter Bedell Smith

Henry DeWolf Smyth

WILLIAM COOPER: DEATH OF A CONSPIRACY SALESMAN

Shields Warren

Carroll L. Wilson

Arnold Wolfers

The second phase meetings were also held at the Marine Base at Quantico Virginia and the group became known as Quantico II.

Nelson Rockefeller built a retreat somewhere in Maryland which could only be reached by air for MJ-12 and the study committee so that they could meet away from public scrutiny. This secret meeting place is known by the code name "The Country Club". Complete living, eating, recreation, library, and meeting facilities exist at the location.

The study group was "publicly" closed in the later months of 1958 and Henry Kissinger published what was officially termed the results in 1957 as "Nuclear Weapons and Foreign Policy" by Henry A. Kissinger, published for the Council on Foreign Relations by Harper & Brothers, New York. In truth the manuscript had already been 80% written while Kissinger was at Harvard. The study group continued veiled in secrecy.

A clue to the seriousness Kissinger attached to the study can be found in statements by his wife and friends. Many of them stated that Henry would leave home early each morning and return late each night without speaking to anyone or responding to anyone. It seemed as if he were in another world which held no room for anyone else.

These statements are very revealing. The revelations of the alien presence and actions during the study must have been a great shock. Henry Kissinger was definitely out of character during time surrounding these meetings. He would never again be affected in this manner no matter the seriousness of any subsequent event. On many occasions he would work very late into the night after having already put in a full day. This behavior eventually led to divorce.

A major finding of the alien study was that the public could not be told as it was believed that this would most certainly lead to economic collapse, collapse of the religious structure, and national panic which would lead into anarchy. Secrecy thus continued.

An offshoot of this finding was that if the public could not be told then the Congress could not be told, thus funding for the projects and research would have to come from outside the government. In the meantime, money was to be obtained from the military budget and from CIA confidential non-appropriated funds.

Genetic Experimentation

Another major finding was the aliens were using humans and animals for a source of glandular secretions, enzymes, hormonal secretions, blood, and in horrible genetic experiments. The aliens explained these actions as necessary to their survival. They stated that their genetic structure had deteriorated and that they were no longer able to reproduce. They stated that if they were unable to improve their genetic structure their race would soon cease to exist.

We looked upon their explanations with extreme suspicion. Since our weapons were literally useless against the aliens, MJ-12 decided to continue friendly diplomatic relations with them until such time as we were able to develop a technology which would enable us to challenge them on a military basis.

Overtures would have to be made to the Soviet Union, and other nations, to join forces for the survival of humanity. In the meantime plans were developed to research and construct two weapons systems using conventional and nuclear technology which would hopefully bring us to parity. The results of the research were Projects JOSHUA and EXCALIBUR.

Joshua was a weapon captured from the Germans that at that time was capable of shattering 4" thick armor plate at a range of two miles using low frequency sound waves, and it was believed that this weapon would be effective against the alien craft and beam weapons.

Excalibur was a weapon carried by missile not to exceed 30,000 feet AGL, not to deviate from designated target more than 50 meters, would penetrate 1,000 meters of tufa hard packed soil such as that found in New Mexico, would carry a one megaton warhead, and was intended for use in destroying the aliens in their underground bases.

Joshua was developed successfully but never used to my knowledge. Excalibur was not pushed until recent years and now there is an unprecedented effort to develop this weapon.

WILLIAM COOPER: DEATH OF A CONSPIRACY SALESMAN

The events at Fatima in the early part of the century were scrutinized. On suspicion that it was alien manipulation, an intelligence operation was put into motion to penetrate the secrecy surrounding the event. The United States utilized its Vatican moles that had been recruited and nurtured during WWII and soon obtained the entire Vatican study which included the prophecy.

This prophecy stated that if man did not turn from evil and place himself at the feet of Christ the planet would self-destruct and the events described in the book of Revelations would indeed come to pass. It stated that a child would be born who would unite the world with a plan for world peace and a false religion beginning in 1992.

By 1995 the people would discern that he was evil and was indeed the Anti-Christ. World War III would begin in the Middle East in 1995 with an invasion of Israel by a United Arab nation using conventional weapons which would culminate in a nuclear holocaust in the year 1999.

Between 1999 and 2003 most of the life on this planet would suffer horribly and die as a result. The return of Christ would occur in the year 2011.

When the aliens were confronted with this finding they confirmed that it was true. The aliens explained that they had created us through hybridization and had manipulated the human race through religion, Satanism, witchcraft, magic, and the occult. They further explained that they were capable of time travel and the events would indeed come to pass.

Later exploitation of alien technology by the United States and the Soviet Union utilizing time travel confirmed the prophecy. The aliens showed a hologram which they claimed was the actual crucifixion of Christ, which the government filmed. We did not know whether to believe them or not.

Were they using genuine religions to manipulate us, or were they indeed the source of our religions with which they had been manipulating us all along? On the other hand, was this the beginning of the genuine end times and the return of Christ, which was predicted in the Bible? No one knew the answer.

A symposium was held in 1957 that was attended by some of the greatest scientific minds then living. They reached the conclusion that by or shortly after the year 2000 the planet would self destruct due to increased population and man's exploitation of the environment without any help from God or the aliens.

Alternatives 1, 2, and 3

By secret Executive Order of President Eisenhower, the Jason Scholars were ordered to study this scenario and make recommendations called "Alternatives 1, 2, and 3".

"Alternative 1" was to use nuclear devices to blast holes in the stratosphere from which the heat and pollution would escape into space. Change the human cultures from that of exploitation into cultures of environmental protection. Of the three this was decided to be the least likely to succeed due the inherent nature of man and the additional damage the nuclear explosions would themselves create.

"Alternative 2" was to build a vast network of underground cities and tunnels in which a select representation of all cultures and occupations would survive and carry on the human race. The rest of humanity would be left to fend for themselves on the surface of the planet.

"Alternative 3" was to exploit the alien and conventional technology in order for a select few to leave the Earth and establish colonies in outer space. I am not able to confirm nor deny the existence of "Batch Consignments" of human slaves which would be used for the manual labor in the effort as part of the plan. The Moon, code named "Adam", would be the object of primary interest followed by the planet Mars, code named "Eve".

As a delaying action, all three alternatives included birth control, sterilization, and the introduction of deadly microbes to control or slow the growth of the Earth's population.

AIDS is only one result of these plans. There are others. It was decided since the population must be reduced and controlled that it would be in the best interest of the human race to rid ourselves of the undesirable elements of our society.

The joint U.S. & Soviet leadership dismissed "Alternative 1" but ordered work to begin on "Alternative 2 and 3" virtually at the same time.

WILLIAM COOPER: DEATH OF A CONSPIRACY SALESMAN

In 1959, the Rand Corporation hosted a Deep Underground Construction Symposium. In the Symposium report, machines are pictured and described which could bore a tunnel 45 feet in diameter at the rate of 5 feet per hour. It also displays pictures of huge tunnels and underground vaults containing what appear to be complex facilities and possibly even cities. It appears that the previous 5 years of all out underground construction had made significant progress by that time.

The ruling powers decided that one means of funding the alien connected and other black market projects was to corner the illegal drug market. A young ambitious member of the Council on Foreign Relations was approached. His name is George Bush who at the time was president and C.E.O. of Zapata Oil based in Texas.

Zapata Oil was experimenting with the new technology of offshore drilling. It was correctly thought that the drugs could be shipped from South America to the offshore platforms by fishing boat where it would then be taken to shore by the normal transportation used for supplies and personnel.

By this method, no customs or law enforcement agency would subject the cargo to search. George Bush agreed to help and organized the operation in conjunction with the CIA. The plan worked better than anyone had thought and has since expanded worldwide and there are now many other methods of bringing the illegal drugs into the country. It must always be remembered though that George Bush began sale of drugs to our children.

The CIA now controls all the world's illegal drug markets.

The REAL Space Program

The "official" space program was boosted by President Kennedy in his inaugural address when he mandated that the United States put a man on the moon before the end of the decade. Although innocent in its conception this mandate enabled those in charge to funnel vast amounts of money into black projects and conceal the REAL space program from the American people.

A similar program in the Soviet Union served the same purpose. In fact a joint alien, United States, and Soviet Union base already existed on the moon at the very moment Kennedy spoke the words. On May 22, 1962 a space probe landed on Mars and confirmed the existence of an environment which could support life. Not long afterward the construction of a colony on the planet Mars began in earnest.

Today cities exist on Mars populated by specifically selected people from different cultures and occupations taken from all over the Earth.

A public charade of antagonism between the Soviet Union and the United States has been maintained over all these years in order to fund projects in the name of National Defense when in fact we are the closest allies.

Kennedy Assassination

At some point, President Kennedy discovered portions of the truth concerning the drugs and the aliens. He issued an ultimatum in 1963 to MJ-12. President Kennedy assured them that if they didn't clean up the drug problem he would. He informed MJ-12 that he intended to reveal the presence of aliens to the American people within the following year and ordered a plan developed to implement his decision.

President Kennedy was not a member of the Council on Foreign Relations and knew nothing of "Alternative 2" or "Alternative 3". Internationally the operations were supervised by MJ-12 and in the Soviet Union by its sister organization. President Kennedy's decision struck fear into the hearts of those in charge. His assassination was ordered by the Policy Committee and the order was carried out by agents of MJ-12 in Dallas.

President John F. Kennedy was murdered by the Secret Service agent who drove his car in the motorcade and the act is plainly visible in the film. Watch the driver and not Kennedy when you view the film. All of the witnesses who were close enough to the car to see William Greer shoot Kennedy were themselves all murdered within the next two years of the event.

The Warren Commission was a farce and Council on Foreign Relations members made up the majority of its panel. They succeeded in snowing the American people. Many other patriots who attempted to reveal the alien secret have also been murdered throughout the intervening years.

During the era of the United States initial space exploration and the Moon landings, every launch was accompanied by alien craft. A Moon base dubbed Luna was sighted and filmed by the Apollo astronauts. Domes, spires, tall round structures which look like silos, huge "T" shaped mining vehicles which left stitch-like tracks in the lunar surface, and extremely large as well as small alien craft appear in the photographs. It is a joint United States, Russian and Alien base.

The Space Program is a farce and unbelievable waste of money. Alternative 3 is a reality and is not at all science fiction. Most of the Apollo astronauts were severely shaken by this experience and their lives and subsequent statements reflect the depth of the revelation and the effect of the muzzle order which followed.

They were ordered to remain silent or suffer extreme penalty, DEATH, which was termed an "expediency". One astronaut actually did talk to the British producers of the TV expose "Alternative 3" confirming many of the allegations.

In the book "*Alternative 003*" the pseudonym "Bob Grodin" was used in place of the astronaut's identity. It was also stated that he committed suicide in 1978. This cannot be validated by any source and I believe that several so-called facts in the book are disinformation. I firmly believe that this disinformation is a result of pressure put upon authors and is meant to nullify the effect upon the populace of the British TV expose entitled "Alternative 3".

The headquarters of the international conspiracy is in Geneva, Switzerland. The ruling body is made up of representatives of the governments involved as well as the executive members of the group known as the "Bilderbergers". Meetings are held by the "Policy Committee" when necessary on a nuclear submarine beneath the polar ice cap.

The secrecy is such that this was the only method which would ensure that the meetings would not be bugged. I can say that the book is at least 70% true from my own knowledge and the knowledge of my sources.

I believe that the disinformation was an attempt to compromise the British TV expose with information which could be proven false, just as the "Eisenhower Briefing Document" was released here in the U.S. under the contingency plan "Majestic Twelve", and which can also be proven false.

Since our interaction with the aliens began we have come into possession of technology beyond our wildest dreams.

A craft named Aurora exists at Area 51 which makes regular trips into space. It is a one stage ship called a TAV (transatmospheric vehicle) and it can take off from the ground using a 7 mile runway, go into high orbit, return on its own power, and land on the same runway. We currently have and fly atomic powered alien type craft at Area S-4 in Nevada.

Our pilots have made interplanetary voyages in these craft and have been to the Moon, Mars, and other planets aboard these craft. We have been lied to about the true nature of the moon, the planets Mars and Venus and the real state of technology that we possess today at this very moment.

There are areas on the moon where plant life grows and even changes color with the seasons. This seasonal effect is because the moon does not, as claimed, always present the exact same side to the Earth or the sun. There is an area that wobbles in and out of darkness on a seasonal basis and it is near this area that the plant life grows.

The moon does have a few man-made lakes and ponds upon its surface and clouds have been observed and filmed in its atmosphere. It possesses a gravitational field and man can walk upon its surface without a space suit breathing from an oxygen bottle after undergoing decompression the same as any deep sea diver. I have seen the photographs and some of them were actually published in the book "We Discovered Alien Bases on the Moon" by Fred Steckling.

In 1969 a confrontation broke out between the human scientists and the aliens at the Dulce underground lab. The aliens took many of our scientists hostage. Delta forces were sent to free them but were no match against the alien weapons. 66 of our people were killed during this action.

As a result we withdrew from all joint projects for at least 2 years. A reconciliation eventually took place and once again we began to interact. Today the alliance continues.

Nixon Forced To Resign

When the Watergate scandal broke, President Nixon had intended to ride out the storm confident that he could not be impeached. MJ-12, however, had a different agenda. The intelligence community rightfully concluded that an impeachment trial would open up the files and bare the awful secrets to the public eye. Nixon was ordered to resign. He refused and so the first military coup ever to take place in the United States was promulgated.

The joint Chiefs of Staff sent a TOP SECRET message to the commanders of all U.S. armed forces throughout the world. It stated, "Upon receipt of this message you will no longer carry out any orders from the White House. Acknowledge receipt."

This message was sent a full 5 days before Nixon conceded and announced publicly that he would resign. I personally saw this message.

When I asked my commanding officer what he would do as obviously the order violated the Constitution, I was told, "I guess I will wait to see if any orders come from the White House and then I will decide."

I did not see any communication from the White House but that does not mean that none was sent.

During all the years that this has been happening the Congress and the American people have seemed to know instinctively that something was not right. When the Watergate scandal surfaced they jumped on the bandwagon and everyone thought that the agencies would be cleaned out.

President Ford organized the Rockefeller commission to do the job. At least that is what everyone thought. His real purpose was to head off the Congress and keep the cover-up going. Nelson Rockefeller who headed the commission investigating the intelligence community was a member of the Council on Foreign Relations and was the one who helped Eisenhower build the MJ-12 power structure. Rockefeller uncovered only enough to keep the hounds at bay.

He threw the Congress few bones and the cover-up rolled merrily along as always.

Later Senator Church would conduct the famous Church hearings. He also was a prominent member of the Council on Foreign Relations and he only repeated the Rockefeller act. Again the cover-up prevailed. When Iran Contra came along we thought this time it had to come gushing out. Wrong again! Despite mountains of documents that pointed to drug smuggling and other hidden monsters, the cover-up sailed through.

Congress even seemed to go out of its way to duck the issues that were just under the surface. Could it be that Congress knows the whole thing and won't touch it? Are they among the select who have been picked for the Mars colony when the Earth begins to destruct?

I cannot even begin to outline the entire financial empire controlled by the CIA, the NSA, and the Council on Foreign Relations that controls and launders money from drugs and intelligence community proprietary ventures but I can tell you the little that I know. The amount of money is beyond anything you can imagine and is hidden in a vast networks of banks and holding companies.

You should first begin to look at, The J. Henry Schroder Banking Corporation; The Schroder Trust Company; Schroders Limited (London); Helbert Wagg Holdings, LTD.; J. Henry Schroder-Wagg & Co., LTD; Schroder Gerbruder and Company (Germany); Schroder Munchmeyer Hengst and Company; Castle Bank and its holding companies; The Asian Development Bank; The Nugan Hand octopus of banks and holding companies.

Contingency Plan

A contingency plan was formulated by MJ-12 to throw everyone off the trail should they come close to the truth. The plan was known as MAJESTIC TWELVE. It was implemented with the release by Moore, Shandera, and Friedman of the purported genuine "Eisenhower Briefing Document". The document is a fraud.

The document lists the Executive Order as #092447. A number which does not exist and will not exist for quite a long time at the present rate. Truman wrote Executive Orders in the 9,000 range, Eisenhower wrote in the 10,000 range, Ford was up to the 11,000 bracket, and Reagan got only into the 12,000 numbers.

Executive Orders are numbered consecutively, no matter who occupies the White House for reasons of continuity, record keeping, and to prevent confusion. The Executive Order is only one of several fatal flaws contained within the document. The plan so far has thrown the entire research community off the trail for several years and has resulted in the wasted expenditure of money looking for information that does not exist.

It resulted in a total waste of a grant by the Fund for UFO Research of $16,000 which was given to Stanton Friedman to research the information. Many thousands of man hours have gone into looking for a "red herring". If you doubt the secret government's ability to run you through the rose garden you had better think again.

Another contingency plan is in force and is working upon you today. It is the plan to prepare the public for eventual confrontation with an alien race. The public is being bombarded with movies, radio, advertising, and TV depicting almost every aspect of the true nature of the alien presence.

This includes the good and the bad. Look around and pay attention. The aliens are planning to make their presence known and the government is preparing you for it so that there will be no panic.

The worst contingency plan has also been implemented and is at work right now. For many years now they have been importing drugs and selling them to the people and mainly the poor and minorities. Social welfare programs were put into place to create a dependent non-working element of our society.

They began to remove the social welfare programs in order to develop a large criminal class that did not exist in the 50's and early 60's. They encouraged the manufacture and importation of deadly military firearms for the criminal element to use. This was intended to foster a feeling of insecurity which would lead the American people to voluntarily disarm themselves by passing laws against firearms. Incidents were to be staged to speed up the process.

By using drugs and hypnosis in a process called Orion on mental patients the CIA inculcated the desire in these people to open fire on school yards and inflame the anti-gun lobby. This plan is well underway and so far is working as planned. This plan must not succeed.

Martial Law and Concentration Camps

Due to the wave of crime sweeping the nation they will convince the American people a state of anarchy exists within the major cities. They are now building their case almost nightly on TV and daily in newspapers. When public opinion has been won over to this idea they intend to state that a terrorist group armed with a nuclear weapon has entered the United States and that they plan to detonate this device in one of our cities.

WILLIAM COOPER: DEATH OF A CONSPIRACY SALESMAN

The government will then suspend the Constitution and declare martial law. The secret alien army of implanted humans and all dissidents, which translated into anyone they choose, will be rounded up and will be placed in concentration camps which already exist throughout the country. They are each one mile square.

Are the people whom they intend to place in these concentration camps destined to make the reported "Batch Consignments" of slave labor needed by the space colonies? The media, radio, TV, newspapers, and computer networks will be nationalized and seized. Anyone who resists will be taken or killed. This entire operation was rehearsed by the government and military in 1984 under the code name REX-84 and it went off without a hitch.

When these events have transpired the secret government and/or alien takeover will be complete. Your freedom will never be returned and you will live in slavery for the remainder of your life. You had better wake up and you had better do it now.

Secret Government Agents

Phil Klass is an agent of the CIA and this was stated in the documents I saw between 1970 and 1973. One of his jobs as an aviation expert was to debunk everything to do with UFOs. All military commanders were instructed to call him to gain information on how to debunk and/or explain UFO contacts and/or sightings to the public and/or press if and when the need arose.

William Moore, Jaimie Shandera, and Stanton Friedman are either witting (with knowledge) or unwitting (being used without knowledge) agents of the secret government. I prefer to believe that they are unwitting although William Moore's reported us of a Defense Investigation Service ID card and his reported self confession to Lee Graham that he was an agent of the government makes me seriously doubt it, if the reports are true. Lee Graham called me at my home, and when asked, he confirmed that Moore had indeed done this.

Stanton Friedman has told me and many others that years ago he, "helped develop a nuclear reactor, to power an aircraft that was the size of a basketball, was clean, turned out hydrogen, and worked like a dream".

His words not mine. The only fuel which could go into such an engine and produce hydrogen as a byproduct is water. The only place in the universe at that time to get such technology was from the aliens. Is he really unwitting? I do not know. He was a member of the Moore, Shandera, and Friedman research team and it was they who implemented the MAJESTIC TWELVE contingency plan.

In the documents which I saw between 1970 and 1973 names of individuals were listed who were to be targeted for recruitment in order that the contingency plan known as MAJESTIC TWELVE could be introduced to the public by persons known and respected by the public.

Bruce Macabee, Stanton Friedman, and William Moore were among those listed. I do not know that the subsequent events do not seem to indicate the Bruce Macabee is involved but the actions of Stanton Friedman and William Moore are highly suspect.

I know that all the major UFO research organizations were targeted for infiltration and control by the secret government just as NICAP was infiltrated and controlled. I believe that these efforts have been successful. It is very possible that the major UFO publications are also controlled.

Majestic 12 Today

Today, MJ-12 still exists and operates just as it always has. It is made up of the same structure, six from the same positions in government, and six from the executive members of the Council on Foreign Relations and/or Trilateral Commission. The Majority Agency for Joint Intelligence is publicly known as the Senior Interagency Group (SIG).

In closing, it is most important to understand that the Council on Foreign Relations and its offshoot the Trilateral Commission not only control but own this country. Long before WWII they were instrumental in helping to decide policy for the United States government.

The Council on Foreign Relations, Trilateral Commission and their foreign counterparts report to Bilderbergers. Almost every high level government and military official of any consequence since WWII including presidents have been members of the Council on Foreign Relations and/or Trilateral Commission. All American members of the Trilateral Commission have either been or are a member of the Council on Foreign Relations.

Each foreign nation of any importance has its own offshoot of the Council on Foreign Relations and the members of each country interact with those of other countries through the Bilderbergers to further their common goals. The foreign member of the Trilateral Commission belong to their respective organizations.

Even a cursory investigation by the most inexperienced researcher will show that the members of the Council on Foreign Relations and the Trilateral Commission control: the major foundations; all of the major media; publishing interests; the largest banks; all the major corporations; the upper echelons of the government; many other vital interests...

Their members are elected and appointed because they have all the money and special interests behind them. All, that is, except the peoples. They are undemocratic and do not in any way represent the majority of the U.S. of America. These are the people who will decide who survives the coming holocaust and who does not.

The Bilderbergers, the Council on Foreign Relations and the Trilateral Commission are the secret government and rule this nation through MJ-12 and the study group known as the Jason Society or Jason Scholars and the top echelon of the government which consist mostly of their members.

Alien Manipulation

Throughout our history the aliens have manipulated and/or ruled the human race through various secret societies, religion, magic, witchcraft, and the occult. The Council on Foreign Relations and the Trilateral Commission are in complete control of the alien technology and are also in complete control of the nation's economy.

Eisenhower was the last president to know the entire overview of the alien problem. Succeeding presidents were told only what MJ-12 and the Intelligence Community wanted them to know and believe me, it wasn't the truth.

MJ-12 has presented each new president with a picture of a lost alien culture seeking to renew itself, build a home on this planet, and shower us with gifts of technology. In some cases the president was told nothing. Each president in turn has bought the story, or no story at all, hook line and sinker.

WILLIAM COOPER: DEATH OF A CONSPIRACY SALESMAN

Meanwhile innocent people continue to suffer unspeakable horrors at the hands of alien and human scientists who are engaged in barbarous research that would make even the Nazis look like Sunday school children. As if that is not enough many people end up as food for the insatiable alien appetite for biological enzymes, glandular hormonal secretions, and blood.

Many people are abducted and are sentenced to live with psychological and physical damage for the rest of their lives. In the documents I saw, 1 in 40 humans have been implanted with devices the purpose of which I have never discovered. The government believes that the aliens are building an army of human implants which can be activated and turned upon us at will. You should also know that to date we have not even begun to come close to parity with the aliens.

Is this technology worth it? The conclusions are inescapable:

The secret power structure believes that, because of our own ignorance or by Divine Decree, planet Earth will self destruct sometime in the near future. These men sincerely believe that they are doing the right thing in their attempt to save the human race. It is terribly ironic that they have been forced to take as their partner an alien race which is itself engaged in a monumental struggle for survival.

Many moral and legal compromises have been made in this joint effort. These compromises were made in error and must be corrected and those responsible should be made to account for their actions. I can understand the fear and urgency that must have been instrumental in the decision not to tell the public. Obviously I disagree with this decision.

Throughout history small but powerful groups of men have consistently felt that they alone were capable of deciding the fates of millions and throughout history they have been wrong. This great nation owes its very existence to the Principles of Freedom and Democracy.

I believe with all my heart that the United States of America cannot and will not succeed in any effort that ignores those principles. Full disclosure to the public should be made and we should proceed to save the human race altogether.

WILLIAM COOPER: DEATH OF A CONSPIRACY SALESMAN

We are being manipulated by a joint human/alien power structure which will result in the total enslavement and or destruction of the human race. The government has been totally deceived and we are being manipulated by an alien power which will result in the total enslavement and/or destruction of the human race. We must use any and every means available to prevent this from happening.

Something else is happening which is beyond our ability to understand at this time. We must force disclosure of all the facts, discover the truth and act upon the truth.

In any case we MUST force disclosure of the truth or no matter what happens we will surely deserve it. The situation in which we find ourselves is due to our own actions or inactions over the last 44 years. It is our own fault and we are the only ones who can change it.

Through ignorance or misplaced trust we as a people have abdicated our role as the "watch dog" of our government. Our government was founded "of the people, for the people, by the people". There was no mention or intent to ever abdicate our role and place our total trust in a handful of men who meet secretly and decide our fate for us. In fact the structure of our government was designed to prevent that from ever happening. If we had done our jobs as citizens this could never have happened.

Most of us are completely ignorant as to even the most basic functions of our government. We have truly become a nation of sheep. Sheep are always eventually led to the slaughter. It is time to stand up in the manner of our forefathers and walk like men.

I remind you all, that the Jews of Europe marched to the ovens, after having been warned, believing all the while that the facts could not possibly be true. When the outside world was told of the holocaust occurring in Hitler's Europe it was not believed. I state here and now that Hitler was manipulated by these same aliens.

I have brought you the truth as I know it. I do not care what you think of me. I have done my duty and no matter what fate lies in store for me, I can truly meet my maker with a clear conscience.

WILLIAM COOPER: DEATH OF A CONSPIRACY SALESMAN

"The reason I go about it the way I do is that this is the only way to shock people awake. We're at the point now where the only thing that will work is a slap upside the head - and at times I wish I could do it physically. If I did, I would go to jail; so I slap people mentally and say 'WAKE UP'...this is what is happening! If I stood up there and was real nice, nobody would listen."
William Cooper

WILLIAM COOPER: DEATH OF A CONSPIRACY SALESMAN

WRITE US FOR OUR FREE CATALOG:

GLOBAL COMMUNICATIONS
P.O. BOX 753
NEW BRUNSWICK, NJ 08903

(DON'T FORGET TO INCLUDE YOUR NAME AND MAILING ADDRESS)

E-MAIL: MRUFO8@HOTMAIL.COM

WWW.CONSPIRACYJOURNAL.COM

www.ingramcontent.com/pod-product-compliance
Lightning Source LLC
Chambersburg PA
CBHW081417270326
41931CB00015B/3307